'Tell me about the Holy Spirit'

In memory of my sister Eileen,
who watched over me for many years with love

Inigo Text Series: 13

'Tell me about the Holy Spirit'

Eye-opener and Ear-opener

Gerald O'Mahony, S.J.

GRACEWING

First published in 2012
jointly by

Gracewing
2 Southern Avenue
Leominster
Herefordshire
HR6 0QF

Inigo Enterprises
Links View
Traps Lane
New Malden
Surrey
KT3 4RY

'The expense is reckoned; the enterprise is begun.
It is of God ...'

Cover design based on 'Spirit' by Norman Dilworth
Corten steel 2001, 350cm x 280cm

ISBN 978 085244 777 2

Typesetting by
Action Publishing Technology Ltd, Gloucester GL1 5SR

Contents

Introduction

The world of Christians who pray seems to be divided between those for whom the Holy Spirit is everything, and those for whom the Holy Spirit is a puzzle. I am writing for the latter, those who would like to know more about the Spirit, but who do not know where to begin. I obviously cannot claim to have all the answers, but I hope to share what I know to be true. There was a rich man in the parables of Jesus who could not be bothered to share his riches with the poor man Lazarus begging at his gate; I want to share mine with whoever wishes to come closer to the Holy Spirit of God, but who does not seem able to get past the gate.

There are some people who prefer to think God, and in particular the Holy Spirit, can shift reality around if we ask earnestly enough. They belong to the school that takes Jesus literally when he says faith can remove mountains. Others prefer to accept reality for what it is, but would pray to have their eyes opened to see the same reality in a different light. What appeared to be a mountain in my way turns out to be nothing but a molehill when the Holy Spirit shines a light. Then too, Jesus was forever asking people to open their ears and hear him aright. Sayings of Jesus that sound at first like a threat from God (because we are guilty parties) turn out so often to be words of love. As in the fairy tale, Beauty sees a true lover, not a Beast any more, and finally understands the words that are spoken.

My own training in the spiritual life from the age of eleven has been mainly in the footsteps of St Ignatius of Loyola, both when I was a schoolboy in secondary education and in my training and practice as a Jesuit. There will, accordingly, be evidence of that in the way I trace what may be said about the Holy Spirit. Perhaps my only original way of treating the matter of the Spirit will be the way I divide the gospel into the realm of sheep and the realm of shepherds, and see there an echo of the way the Holy Spirit proceeds from the Father and from the Son ... but much more of that in its proper place.

Not all that long ago I wrote a book of bidding prayers for the three years of the Sunday liturgy (*The Prayer of the Faithful* Kevin Mayhew, 2007), and I was conscious of two things in the writing of it: one, that I was not mentioning the Holy Spirit by name anything like as much as the other two Persons of the Trinity, and two, that the Spirit never stopped opening my eyes and ears as the writing went along. Perhaps now I can restore the balance a little, and talk about the Holy Spirit directly.

1

'When the wind blows ...'

When a human baby is born, it has never breathed in or breathed out. There was no free air in the womb, and life came along by other means. So which happens first, breathing in or breathing out? It has to be breathing in, since the baby had no breath in its lungs ready for breathing out. Baby breathes in, then breathes out, usually with a cry of alarm that gives huge satisfaction to everyone within earshot: the baby is alive.

'Spirit' is a word that comes from ancient Latin, meaning 'breath' or 'wind' or 'breeze'. In treatises on the Holy Trinity, the Holy Spirit is the name used for the breath of love that comes freely from God to another Person in God, who owns it, breathes it in, then breathes it back again with gratitude. Even that Second Person could not have breathed out without first breathing in. God the First Person is the one and only Person, ever, who could breathe out love without first breathing love in. God the First Person alone is love without having first been loved. God the First Person alone is the fire that nobody lit, the rock that rests on no other.

Jesus one time told Nicodemus, the man who came to Jesus by night so as to keep his visit secret, how the wind blows wherever it wants to; we can hear the sound of it, but we do not know where it comes from, nor where it is going. We believe something very similar to that about the Holy Spirit. We cannot see the Spirit; it comes and goes according to its own plan, but we feel its presence. We do however know where the Spirit comes from, since it is the breath of God; we also know where the Spirit is going next, namely back to God, sent or breathed back by the Second Person. I sometimes compare what happens when two magnets cling to one another: there is one magnet and there is another magnet, and between them is a magnetism. The First Person is like one magnet, the Second Person like another magnet, and the Spirit is like the magnetism. Where the comparison falls down is that in God there is only One first source from which Love goes out to Another, then the Love comes back again from the Other to the One where Love started. In God the Love has but one beginning and end; magnetism in the example I am using just goes round and round. In God the first Love brought the other Love (Love-in-return-for-love) into being.

I have been calling the Spirit 'it', in the same sort of way one might call Love 'it' even though all love is so very personal. I will come back in another chapter to the way we sometimes give the Holy Spirit a seeming gender, a 'he' or a 'she'. On the one hand, speaking as we Christians do about God as Father, Son and Holy Spirit, we can more easily picture a father and a son as personal, rather than a spirit, which sounds more disembodied. Yet looked at another way, surely the Holy Spirit is the most personal to human thinking, since according to Jesus the Spirit reaches from the innermost depths of the Father's mind and heart to the innermost mind and heart of Jesus, and back again. We call personal not the mere presence of somebody, but rather whether they reveal to us something of what they are thinking or feeling.

There is a strange fact about official Catholic prayers, as found in the liturgical books: the prayers are addressed ninety-eight percent of the time to the Father, the First Person, through the Son, the Second Person. Two percent or thereabouts are spoken to the Son. None of them is addressed to the Holy Spirit. Hymns, yes, and canticles, but no formal prayers: no Opening Prayers, no Prayers over the Gifts, no Prayers after Communion, no Eucharistic Prayers, not even on feasts or celebrations of the Holy Spirit. All I wish to do here and now is to note the fact, because the fact in itself is going to be relevant to our understanding of the Holy Spirit. We know Jesus prayed to God as his Abba, his first-generation Father. We know that the Jews in the tradition Jesus came from had prayed always to God, the same God Jesus in his day called 'Abba'; we know that Jesus authorized his disciples to pray to that same God and Abba through him, through Jesus the Son; we know too that shortly after Jesus' death and resurrection his disciples could be found praying to Jesus himself. 'Lord Jesus, receive my soul' was the last prayer of Stephen the first Christian martyr. But nobody seems instinctively to have prayed 'Come, Holy Spirit' until much later in the Church's history, and then only in hymns and canticles. 'Heavenly Father, we pray through Jesus Christ your Son, who lives and reigns with you in the unity of the Holy Spirit' is as close as the Holy Spirit gets to being prayed to. We can begin to wonder why.

If the Holy Spirit is God's love breathed to another person, why is that breath called Holy with a capital H ? We tend to think of holy things as things apart: 'Take off your shoes, Moses; this is holy ground; you do not really belong here'. There is something of 'separate' in most uses of the word 'holy'. But in the context of the Holy Spirit, the word 'holy' means rather 'good all through'. The Holy Spirit puts the very best and kindest and truest interpretation on everything that happens and on everything that is said from one person to another. The Holy Spirit communicates the truth. The Holy Spirit communicates the true goodness of God, from one person to another. The Holy Spirit in fact leads us to see our true selves, not some other reality beyond our reach. The Holy Spirit is a Friend, as promised by Jesus.

The First Person breathes out love to the Second Person, and the Second Person receives the knowledge of being loved. The Second Person loves in return for love, and the First Person knows being loved-in-return. This successful messaging of love between the two cannot be identified with either the First Person or the Second Person. Here the image of two magnets is helpful: the magnetism is not this magnet nor is it the other magnet – it is in both and in between both. In the next chapter I will compare it to homesickness, which belongs here and belongs there, but is not the same thing as here or there. Therefore wise men and women and saints have seen the in-between reality as a Third Person, divine because in God, equal to First and Second in every personal way, but yet different. Three Persons, one God, each Person equal but different: one God: the Beginning of Love, and the Return of Love, and all places In Between.

Wise men and wise women have found that the three Persons in God relate to one another variously within the mystery which is 'God'; but when they work outside the Godhead with us creatures they work as one – as you would expect in a divine loving being. To avoid confusion, we should remember that when the New Testament talks about God, just like that, the writer nearly always means God the First Person. Jesus in turn is called the Christ, the Son of God, or the Christ, the Lord. He is God, he is divine, but he is not the Father. The Holy Spirit is called the Spirit, and is God, is divine, but is not the Father nor the Son. When Father, Son or Spirit deal with us humans, they are in it together.

Christians do not have a monopoly of the Holy Spirit. The Spirit is at work in each and every being on earth that ever was or will be. As Christians we have a framework of wisdom and memory and centuries of prayer behind us, but the system does not define the Spirit nor limit the power of the Spirit to move where it will. 'When the wind blows, the cradle will rock', as the nursery rhyme *Rock-a-bye Baby* reminds us. Every babe on earth will rock to the breeze of God's love, if the rest of us do not get in the way.

This has been rather a heavy first chapter, but I am only introducing the ideas it contains, and I hope to come back to most of them at more leisure. To avoid leaving the Holy Spirit in the head rather than in the heart as well, I hope to close each chapter with a prayer, not necessarily to the Holy Spirit, but with the Holy Spirit in mind.

Prayer for an open mind and heart: *God of surprises, First Person God, your Son Jesus was forever asking his listeners to open their ears, and his audiences to open their eyes to what was already there, but they could not see it. May we not complain that you are asleep. Send your Holy Spirit to open our eyes and our ears to hear and see that you are very much aware of our predicament, and that your help is there for the taking. We ask this through Jesus your Son, who told us to pray to you like this. Amen.*

2

Homesickness

The first and greatest moment of insight I ever had into the way of the Trinity happened while I was praying the Stations of the Cross. I have told this tale in two books before, but it is a very simple way of coming to understand the Holy Spirit, so I will tell it again here. The Stations of the Cross are usually fourteen pictures or relief statues placed in succession on the interior walls of Catholic churches, depicting certain moments of Jesus' final hours. They start with his condemnation by Pilate, and end with his burial. These days they often include a Fifteenth Station, for the Resurrection of Jesus.

I was praying my way round the Stations in the chapel of the college where I was studying philosophy, in semi-darkness because I knew my way around and there was no one else in the chapel at the time. The Fifth Station depicts Simon of Cyrene helping Jesus to carry his cross. God as Trinity suddenly made sense to me. There I was at the Fifth Station, struggling with the cross which to me was Philosophy, in order to stay close to Jesus who had called me there. There was a Way ahead that we both were travelling, with ups and downs and ultimately through death to Resurrection and home to God the First Person, the Father, who was waiting there eagerly for our return, at home there beyond the Fourteenth Station. Like the Prodigal Son, we were going home, in our case in response to a loving call.

That loving call was a sign of the presence of the Holy Spirit, making itself felt. It was homesickness. Jesus and I wanted home. Home wanted us. I already knew from having been at boarding school from age eleven that homesickness was not just in me, but was in my parents and brother and sister as well. This new (to me) homesickness for heaven must both be in Jesus-with-me, and in God the Father waiting for us to get safely home. The homesickness was not Jesus, and the home-sickness was not home. But the homesickness was very real. On later reflection I can see that homesickness does not end when we reach home: it appears then as the clinging to home, the desire and determination never to go away again, the sense of belonging.

We are not Jesus, but we are like Jesus in that we come from God and are going back to God. Our hearts are restless for the place we came from. Again thinking of magnets, we are like a bit of metal suddenly able to be magnetized which finds itself clinging to Jesus, so that his homesickness runs in our veins as well. Jesus is the one who knows the Way home, as it were the lead homing pigeon, or the Lamb who bleats loudly till the Shepherd comes to fetch him; we stay close to him and find our way home. Even when Jesus seems not to be around, we have our own instinct for home given to us by Jesus, his Spirit which keeps us keeping on, crying for help either from the One who calls or from Jesus who will lead us there.

St Ignatius Loyola in his classic book of *Spiritual Exercises* puts near the beginning (section 22) a presupposition. The book is a guide for a spiritual director leading another through thirty days of prayer according to a special pattern. Director and retreatant are going to meet one another for up to one hour each day. Ignatius presupposes that each of the two as good Christians will put the very best possible construction on every-thing the other says, being more ready to do that than to condemn without kindly investigation as to what was really meant. The times when the *Exercises* were written were rife with suspicion about heresy: Ignatius himself was arrested more than once and held on suspicion of heresy: that very fact made him decide to study Latin, philosophy and theology, apply for ordination as a priest, and get a license to teach. Once he had his license he still used the same *Exercises* he started out with, but now he had the qualifications people would trust.

The presupposition is concise, but very far reaching. Think of the Book of Genesis: what a difference if Adam and Eve had presupposed that God meant well by telling them not to eat fruit from the one tree in the middle of the garden! Ignatius himself once called ingratitude the origin of all sin and the greatest of all evils, and really ingratitude is a failure to judge people's good will by the love and gifts they have already given us. A forest of trees in Paradise, and yet according to the story Adam and Eve could not presuppose God really loved them.

There is a wonderful parable in one of the old Laurel and Hardy short films. Somewhere in the archives of film will be found their tale of *The Christmas Tree Sellers*. Stan Laurel and Oliver Hardy have a lorry-load of Christmas trees, and they are going from house to house in December hoping to sell them. They come to a house, drag a tree up the front steps and knock at the door. The householder comes out, hates hawkers, says 'Not today!' and slams the door. The tip of the Christmas tree is trapped in the top of the front door. The two salesmen look at each other, and then knock at the door again, so as to be able to release the tree.

The householder thinks the two are just being rudely persistent, and slams the door even quicker and harder than last time – leaving the tip of the tree again caught in the door. When they knock a third time (after deep thought) he comes out and damages the tree, then slams the door. In retaliation, Laurel and Hardy then damage his house. I forget where they started, on the door itself, or a window, maybe. Revenge leads to more revenge, and at the end of the short film the lorry and all its trees are destroyed, and the house is a ruin! And all for want of a willingness to suppose the other person means well. They meant well with their sales pitch. He was understandably reluctant to have hawkers on his doorstep coming up to Christmas. The tip of the tree getting stuck in the door was simply an accident. If he had not jumped to the conclusion that they were being unreasonable, it could all have been sorted out amicably.

> God as Trinity is unconditional love and forgiveness
> received and understood by Another
> gratefully returned, with no conditions
> and the return of love arrives safely.

Given an impossible scenario, we would have the Father loving the Son, but unable to tell him so or convince him that he was loved. Or, if the first love did reach the target, then the Father would never know if the Son was grateful or not. This is the sort of thing that happens all the time between parents and children, between friends and between lovers, but it is not what happens in God. In God there is the Holy Spirit who makes sure the Second Person knows being loved, and who makes sure the First Person knows being loved-in-return. Loved and forgiven. There might seem to be no need to bring in forgiveness to the Trinity, but there is no such thing as unconditional love without unconditional forgiveness built in. Surely, Jesus on the cross is giving us a true picture of God's Unconditional Love, with forgiveness at the heart of it. It cannot be that the Trinity only invented forgiveness when human beings turned out to be disobedient. Just as homesickness does not stop when all the children are back home, so does homesickness exist before ever the children leave home.

Such, then is the messenger, the communicator of love and understanding, that the world so badly needs. The Laurel and Hardy story of the Christmas tree is a parable of so many bitter quarrels in our lives that could all have been avoided if at the start we had only stopped and looked at things from the point of view of the other party. Quarrels escalate, they start as a stream, grow to a river and end as a raging torrent. When we pray for the Holy Spirit we pray first of all for the vision to see the other point of view; then if, sadly, the quarrel does escalate, we pray for the gift of forgiveness to break through on both sides.

Prayer to know when someone else means well: *God of love, God First Person, please send your Holy Spirit into our meetings with other people. May we learn to take it for granted that those we meet mean well, or are at least doing what they think is right. If relationships sadly go sour, may we make room for forgiveness. We ask this through Jesus the Second Person, who is our constant friend, who hears your voice always and knows its true meaning. Amen.*

3

The Dove

Why is the Holy Spirit said to come down upon Jesus at his baptism in the form of a dove? Pure white doves are very pretty, much more so than their town and country cousins the pigeons, but there is a much better reason than that. In the Book of Genesis Chapter Eight, in the story of Noah and the Ark, the dove has a central role which later makes perfect sense of the dove in the account of Jesus' baptism by John in the Jordan. In the Noah story, when the waters of the flood are receding, Noah sends out a raven through the skylight, and the raven which is quite happy with carrion never comes back. Then Noah sends out the dove, but the dove being more dainty flies around and then returns to the Ark. There is nowhere to rest, nowhere to nest.

Later Noah sends out the dove again, and this time the dove comes back with the leaf of an olive tree in its beak, or maybe it was a small olive branch. The message, all in mime, says, 'Things are growing again out there. The flood is over, and Spring is coming. I can go and make a nest now, and you and Mrs Noah and the family can go out soon onto dry land and start again.' And with that the dove flies off.

What happens in Jesus' baptism puts the Holy Spirit as dove in just the same position as Noah's dove. Coming down onto Jesus, or into Jesus, the dove is saying, 'The flood of God's anger for humankind is not there any more (if it ever was there). I bring an olive branch of peace and friendliness from God: see, the heavens are wide open. In you, Jesus, the human race can come out of prison and start again. Listen;

God says you are his beloved Son. God's favour rests on you, and will never go away.'

This, we are told in three of the four Gospels, is what Jesus saw and experienced in his baptism by John the Baptist. The experience corresponded to the way Jesus in his lifetime spoke to God as 'Abba', meaning 'You are my first-generation Father whose love I can trust for ever. I am your beloved Son, and you are well pleased with me, not for anything I have done or not done, but simply because I am yours.' This is at the heart of any Christian baptism: the Dove settles on the one baptized, and confers the right to call God the First Person 'Abba' as Jesus does. 'I am not in prison any longer, because now I am your beloved daughter (or son), and you are well pleased with me, not for anything I have done or not done, but simply because I am yours.' This is a relationship open to every human being, if only someone could tell every human being that they are already reconciled with God. St Paul twice calls the Holy Spirit the spirit of adoption, by which we call God 'Abba'. This is the Spirit Paul spent the second half of his life trying to spread among the pagans, wherever he found persons willing and able to believe.

The Dove is the spirit of unconditional love and unconditional forgiveness, such as good parents have for their own beloved children. Love and forgiveness with no conditions can be guaranteed in the First Person since we see them in the Second Person who is the reflection of the First Person. The veil keeping us away from the Holy of Holies, that is, from the presence of God the First Person, was torn apart when Jesus died. Jesus himself died praying his Father for unconditional forgiveness to be shown to his murderers. He had just promised Paradise to a thief who had done most of the wrong things in life and failed to do most of the right things. The Dove can reconcile even the greatest of sinners with God, because God as Trinity is none other than love and forgiveness given and received, with full knowledge and consent.

We discover the Trinity at work not 'out there somewhere' apart from ourselves. The Three Persons are at work on ourselves: One calling home, a Second saying, 'Come on, let's go', and a Third saying, 'This means you: you are truly loved, and Jesus will lead you home.' The Holy Spirit is two directional, bringing in the love of the First Person and then helping us first of all to believe in that love as something that belongs there in our heart, and to believe with simple gratitude and praise, no other response necessary. God loves; I believe. This really is God adopting me as son or daughter, with the same intensity of affection as the Father's love for the Son.

For the prayer belonging to this chapter on the Dove, I will offer an imaginative contemplation based on the baptism of Jesus as told in Mark and Luke, with the conversation between Jesus and John the Baptist as told in Matthew's Gospel. I have used this with hundreds of men and women and young people on retreat at the retreat house where I live and work, and the only place in the prayer where anyone gets stuck is in trying to hear God saying to them, 'I am well pleased with you'. This can be felt to be impossible. Then it is good to remember that Jesus himself calls the Spirit 'the Advocate'. An advocate is a lawyer for the defence. When we stand before God to be judged, if we call God 'Lord' and 'Master' and introduce as our defence all the good we ever did, that is not the point. Nothing we ever did would deserve eternal life; there is no way we can earn heaven. But then our Advocate tells us the proper plea: 'Say, "Abba! Forgive me; your child has come home!" and God will embrace you. Only then are you on right terms with God.'

A Gospel contemplation: the baptism of Jesus as a model for my own baptism. Imagine you are a friend of Jesus in Nazareth, before he became famous – Jesus wants to go and see what John the Baptist has started doing – a few of you (friends) want to go with Jesus – Jesus shuts up the carpenter's shop, says au revoir to Mary.

The walk, three days or more – Good weather? – rocky, hilly, or smooth? – Nights in an inn, or camping?

The river Jordan – somewhat carnival atmosphere – queue waiting to be baptized – Jesus and you join the queue – all are asking for the forgiveness of their sins – John sees Jesus in the queue, wants to change places with him, to be baptized by Jesus – Jesus refuses, wanting to be with the sinners.

Jesus is baptized: he sees the heavens split open, nothing between Jesus and God – the Dove comes down, with clear echoes of Noah story – there comes a voice from heaven, from God the origin of love: 'You are my Son, the Beloved; I am well pleased with you, and my favour rests on you, does not go away.'

Then Jesus comes out of the water, says to you, 'I want you to go in next, and see what I saw.' – John baptizes you, heavens split open, nothing between you and God – Holy Spirit comes on you, like a dove, Noah's dove – The voice from heaven calls you by name, says, 'You are my beloved son/daughter; with you I am well pleased – my favour rests on you, does not go away.' – You come up out of the river, to be welcomed by Jesus.

You go back home, never to be the same again, either remembering what God said to you, or else turning it into a statement of faith: 'I am your beloved daughter (beloved son); you are well pleased with me, not for what I have done or failed to do, but simply because I am your own beloved child, and for ever.'

Now that I believe, I will sing forever of your love.

4

True Self

The Holy Spirit is the wind that blows from God, but that is not the only wind that blows. Each of us is like a small boat or a bigger boat, out on the ocean and depending on the winds to get us to where we want to go. Imagine for a moment being out at sea in a yacht with no engine, just sails. If there is no wind at all, I will go nowhere, or be at the mercy of the currents at work in the water. As the wind quickens, I can take control of the yacht, and use the sails to make it go where I want. If then the wind grows even stronger, as a good sailor I reef in the sails to make them smaller and keep control. If the wind becomes a hurricane, my small boat will probably be broken to bits. There is a wind scale: no wind, enough wind, the perfect wind for my craft, and too much wind. What I will be saying is that the Holy Spirit tells me when I have found the perfect wind for my craft. Other winds are either suspect or downright dangerous.

I am talking in pictures, but suppose we stay with this image of the boat for now. How can a sailor change the wind, so that his yacht gets the perfect wind? If there is no wind at all, such a sailor would have to sit tight and wait for one, or else radio for help. Simple sailors used to whistle to encourage a wind to come. In human terms a person in deep desolation or depression is like a craft on the ocean with no wind at all in the sails: such a person can only let time be the healer, or else ask for medical help. A sailor with a light breeze can get going and go looking for a better breeze. A person coming out of depression can begin to work off the depression by doing easier tasks that bring confidence to do more.

If then a storm-force wind comes along, a sensible sailor will shorten sail; a sensible person in a crisis situation will not try to do everything at once but will ease off from inessentials so as to concentrate on essentials. In a threatened hurricane a sailor will send out Mayday signals and batten down the hatches; faced with a crisis beyond the possible, a sensible person asks urgently for help, and will usually stop doing whatever was stirring up the storm, concentrating on survival.

Somewhere in between the two extremes of the doldrums and the hurricane comes the breeze for which my particular craft was designed. A clipper ship would have an ideal wind of a far greater force than a small yacht. But whatever the craft, there is a wind that suits it. Human beings too are every one different, but we each have our ideal amount of stress or 'wind' that gets the best performance out of us. What I am saying about the Holy Spirit is that the Spirit speaks through that perfect wind or stress to each one of us, because the Spirit knows each of us through and through. Winds come and go, but when the right force of wind for my craft comes, the Holy Spirit is the one who is saying, 'This is right; this is you; this is your true self.'

How does anyone relate to a relationship? The Holy Spirit is a relationship. Usually we relate to ordinary persons, to other people: we like them, we resist them, we copy them, or whatever. So how to relate to a personal relationship? The way to relate is by being a channel of the relationship. The Spirit is the relationship between Love and Love-in-return, and that Spirit can either bypass us or flow to and fro within us. If I am out of sorts with myself, I need to manoeuvre myself or go with help either out of the doldrums of depression or back out of the strong winds of over-stress, to reach the 'stillness' of being in the kind of wind I was created for, where my craft, great or small, is perfectly balanced.

The balance in question, for a believer in God, is the balance half way between Love and Love-in-return. These are the two forces that keep me most truly myself. I am loved. I am not unlovable. I am lovable because Someone loves me, and that Someone is the First Person in God. My lovableness has nothing to do with my own actions since I came into the world. If I could make God love me more than God already loves me, then

I would be more powerful than God, which makes nonsense. Then, I am invited to love-in-return, following the example of the Second Person who is Love-in-return-for-love. The most important expression of that love-in-return is simple gratitude: to believe that the love is real, to know where the love comes from, and to say Thank You. Clipper ship or tiny yacht, my perfect progress is a balance between God's goodness and my gratitude.

How can a moving object be called 'still'? I remember when the British aircraft called the Comet first went into commercial use as a passenger plane. The pressmen aboard on the maiden flight were amazed at the stillness of the plane flying at over 400 miles per hour: a twelve-sided threepenny bit would stand on one of its sides on the passenger's table for an hour and not topple over. Or take another metaphor: a spinning top reaches the perfect speed of rotation and seems to stand still. At the circumference it is going very fast, but there is a still point in the centre which is hardly moving at all. When we reach the perfect stress level for our own body and soul, the Holy Spirit calms the very centre of our heart, and tells us we have got things right.

To jump from winds and boats to musical instruments may seem a stretch too far, but there is something about stillness and rightness in many different material things which readily illustrates the movements of the human heart. Take a flute, for instance. Breath is breathed or blown through a flute which sets up resonance in the instrument, and out comes a beautiful sound; but blow too hard and it squeaks, blow too weakly and it does not sound right. The breath of the Spirit, when it matches the true resonance of a human heart, makes music. Take a guitar string or a violin string. Not stretched or stressed enough and the string plucked makes a flat note, if any note at all. Stretched too far or overstressed and the string makes a shrill note and could even snap. Every well-made string created for a musical instrument has a perfect note of its own, when balanced between too slack and too tight. The human heart needs some movement to stay upright, like a child learning to ride a bicycle; but too much movement could lead to loss of control. The Holy Spirit acts as a regulator, saying 'Enough' to our human greed for having too much of everything.

All metaphors aside, what really keeps my heart still and keeps me in my true self is the true balance between being a child of God and being a servant of God. Both are true, but the message from the First Person comes first and takes priority. 'You are my beloved son' or 'You are my beloved daughter' spells my relationship with the First Person, the Father of Jesus. Nothing can take it away, nothing can take away from it. My relationship with the Second Person is to imitate that Person's gratitude at being loved: hence comes thanksgiving, praise, worship, a willingness to think the best of whatever the First Person asks of me. Along with all that comes a security in the love received: no matter how poor my performance, the love will always be there just the same. There lies the key to the Good News brought into the world by Jesus: the love of the First Person is guaranteed, making it safe to love in return.

Whether we are aware of it or not, we are always somewhere between God the First Person and God the Second Person, between the Father and the Son. When we are overstressed or in a hurricane wind, then we are trying to be too close to the First Person, in the sense that we are acting as if we ourselves were God and the ruler of all. At such times everything seems to depend on me, if I am in panic mode; or else everything is dancing to my tune, if I am in manic mode. When on the other hand I am way down depressed, I have forgotten that Someone who is truth itself loves me, regardless of whether I have been a success or failure in the eyes of the world. There is always something precious to be thankful for.

In the middle comes the balance, where I know myself to be a child of God, loved with a parent's love that takes no account of merit. Not every parent is like that, but God the Father is like that, as we know from Jesus his Son. The classical paintings of the baptism of Jesus show the Father above, the Son below, and the Spirit in between.

Prayer to the Holy Spirit: *Holy Spirit of God, who make your way from Father to Son and back again to the Father, teach me the art of balancing between Love and Love-in-return-for-love. Make me enormously grateful for being invited to such a divine situation; make me aware of my own inability to arrive there or to stay there. Open my eyes and my ears, to see love directed at me, and to hear that I am the one being spoken to in love. Teach me to be grateful, and to praise and thank you, and the Father and the Son, and may my gratitude show itself not only in words, but in a determination to show your love in the things I do. Amen.*

5

Two Processions

The title of this chapter sounds as if it is going to be about a carnival, or two carnivals, but No. 'Procession' is a technical term, when it comes to the Holy Spirit. In the ancient fourth-century Creed we find it written that the Holy Spirit proceeds from the Father and from the Son: 'proceeds from', comes out from, is breathed out from, is sent out from. And the sending out is technically known as a procession in the theological language of the time. And in the Trinity there are two of them, two sendings out.

Such at least is the belief of Western Christians united with Rome or stemming from the Church of Rome, though not of Orthodox Christians of Greece and Russia. The Orthodox would prefer to have it that the Holy Spirit proceeds from the Father through the Son, such that only the Father is doing the breathing out, while the Son is more like a channel, not a source, of the Spirit. The difference in belief may seem insignificant, but it was enough to split the early Church in two, and leave two separate models of Christianity ever since.

There is a famous and popular image of the Trinity, a Russian icon by the painter and iconographer Rublev. The faithful in the West are as fond of his painting as anyone else, but many perhaps do not realize that it follows the Eastern understanding of the Trinity, namely just one 'procession'. The Father is on our left as we gaze at the picture, glorious in gold. The Father is looking steadily at the Spirit, who is on our right with garments of blue and green. The Spirit is obediently looking at the cup or chalice in the middle of the table, and offering it to the Son who is seated in the middle behind the table, facing us. The Son looks at the Father with love, and stretches out his hand to accept the cup.

The Spirit is functionally involved in between the Father and the Son, but the Spirit is not involved between the Son and the acceptance of the Father's desire. The story for Rublev goes:

Father – Spirit – Son – Father

whereas for Western theology the story of the Trinity goes

Father – Spirit – Son – Spirit – Father

This may all seem very academic, but in fact there is a very simple way to understand the day-to-day advantages of accepting the Western view. To jump straight to an example: when God loves a sheep of his flock with total love, then asks the sheep to become a shepherd, the Holy Spirit is surely needed both ways. Becoming a shepherd is not a straight extension of being a well-loved sheep. The power to be a shepherd bounces off from Another. The power to be a shepherd proceeds from Another.

I have for many years used a simple diagram to illustrate the way love goes and returns:

(1) God loves   (4) I love

(Spirit)   (Spirit)

(2) I believe   **(3) God invites**

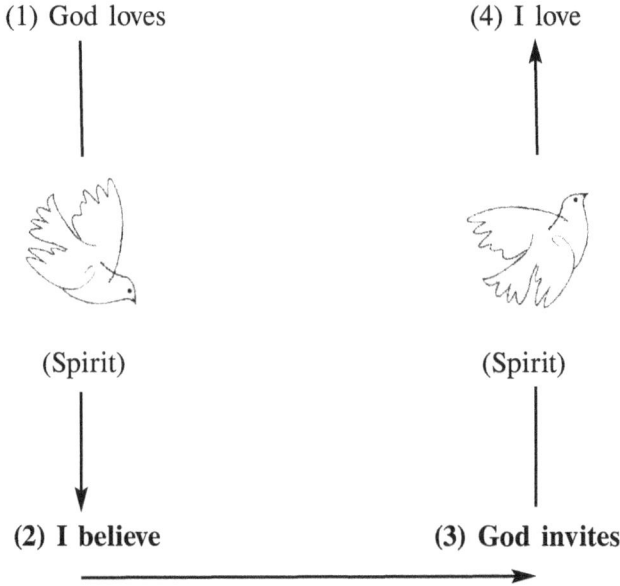

God's love comes first. God sends the Spirit on me, in baptism or in any other loving way, and all I have to do is believe. This establishes me as God's lamb or sheep, loved for no reason but God's reason. The way is then paved for me to love God back, since love calls for love-in-return. However, the sad fact is that alone and unaided I cannot effectively love God back, without a second gift of God. I may be grateful in words, but still find it impossible to put the gratitude into action. Divine actions are beyond me.

The role of the Spirit in even such an everyday transaction as this is in communication. I am first presented with a good thing, but it is the Spirit who tells my heart that the good thing is a gift, and from whom. Then follows an invitation to love in return for the divine gift. Love-in-return-for-love is divine, and belongs to the Second Person of the Trinity, whom we know as Jesus. It is the Second Person who gives us the second gift, of turning gratitude in thought and word to gratitude in deeds. This gift too is of the Spirit, breathed out this time by the Second Person. A lamb loved by God knows what it is to have been loved, and this first-hand knowledge is essential to the transfer-ence to being a shepherd. I am not called to be just any kind of shepherd, but one who loves others, my sheep, in the way I myself was loved and am still loved.

The gospel writers make it clear that knowing the love of God does not translate automatically into loving God back. The Gospel of Mark especially shows Jesus warning his closest disciples time and again that they cannot hope to follow him until such time as he himself will have died and sent them his Spirit. Peter and the others already love him and are grateful to him, that is not the problem. The problem is that they are going to be faced with threats and persecutions and danger of death, and they simply will not be able to be faithful to what they know and believe without the gift of the Spirit, and this is a second gift. They already have faith. They still need inspiration.

The image of sheep and shepherd is especially valuable, since anyone can see it takes a mighty jump from being a lamb to becoming a shepherd (without ceasing to be a lamb). Not all that many years ago there was a happy Australian film entitled *Babe* about a little pig who became a top-class shepherd while remaining a little pig, and the story was clearly a fantasy. What the Holy Spirit does each day is no less wonderful, but real. The same sort of jump is there in other imagery used by Jesus, from being little fish, fished-for, to being a fisher of people, or from being a lost coin to becoming a seeker for coins with the image of God upon them.

Likewise, we cannot become the light of the world unless God's light shines on us, for us to mirror it to others, or unless God lights our candle, for us to hold it up to light everyone in the house. Even then, we need courage beyond what we naturally have, knowing that God's true image is not welcome everywhere. God is an everlasting rock for us, and we cannot become an everlasting rock for others unless we can withstand the storms and tempests God's enemies can throw at us. When Jesus has shown the way, we can know the way but not follow it ourselves, out of fear.

The fundamental image is that of a child of God. I am God's son or God's daughter, beloved for reasons only God knows, and I know and appreciate the gift thanks to the Holy Spirit in my baptism and ever since my baptism. But I do not always behave like a child of God; I do not always put my divine status to one side and work as a servant of God; I am a child of God but I cannot yet do divine deeds; I do not always work and pray to understand what my Father is really like, a Servant; I do not always rely on prayer to see me through the crises that keep cropping up. There is a direct link between the way Jesus prays for hours on end and stays faithful to his Father in the Passion, and the way the Apostles slept through Jesus' agony in the garden only to run away when he was arrested.

The first gift is given freely; the second gift has to be prayed for. Which goes to show the courtesy of our God, in that what is necessary is given freely, whereas what is voluntary (but costly) has to be prayed for.

To go back to the icon of the Trinity by Rublev. People often tell me they see the space in front of them as they view the picture as being a place for themselves to sit and be part of the scene. For myself, I would not like to be sitting there, since all three Persons in the picture are completely taken up with their own concerns and not one of them casts an eye in my direction. An eternity of being ignored would not be my idea of heaven. According to the Western view of the Trinity, however, each of us redeemed by Christ sits with Christ and in Christ, receiving God's love, believing in it, and praying to return it with love-in-return-for-love. The Holy Spirit comes between us and God the First Person in two ways, bringing love from God and returning love to God in union with Jesus. We are not just onlookers, we are partakers.

At this stage I would like to offer a reason why the Church's liturgical prayers speak to the Father through the Son, very occasionally to the Son, but never to the Spirit except in hymns and canticles. The Spirit is always sent. The Spirit only moves at the bidding of Father or Son, so in a way there is no point in praying directly to the Spirit, since the coming of the Spirit will ultimately depend on either the First or the Second Person, or both: unless they send, the Spirit will not come. In terms of processions, the Spirit does not process independently, in either direction. The logical move is to pray to the Father for the knowledge that I am loved, or to pray to the Son for the power to love God back. This can be the theme for the prayer to end the present chapter.

Prayer for the Spirit to be sent: *Heavenly Father, please send the Holy Spirit again, or else let me see more clearly what you have already told me in my baptism – that I am loved by you with an everlasting love as your child. May the Spirit sent again by Jesus inspire in me a great love for you in return, since my entire life and death is in your loving hands. May my love for you be not only in words and feelings, but in actions as well, making light of the difficulties and pains involved, determined to make your name known and loved throughout the world, in imitation of your Son Jesus, in the power of the Holy Spirit. Lord Jesus, I unite my prayers with yours, knowing that they will be answered. Amen.*

6

Baptism and Transfiguration

The Holy Spirit takes a different form in each of these two major events during the life of Jesus, namely his baptism and his transfiguration. In the baptism of Jesus by John the Baptist the Holy Spirit came down on Jesus, or into Jesus perhaps, in the form of a dove. We are inevitably reminded of the dove in the story of Noah and the ark, where the dove is a bringer of an olive branch. Ever since that story was first told, the offering of an olive branch has been a symbol for an offering of peace. When we see the baptism of Jesus as a joint action by all three Persons of the Trinity – the Father acknowledging, the Dove sent with the message, the Son receiving the message – we can interpret the event as depicting the Procession of the Holy Spirit from the Father. The First Person sends a message of unconditional love to the Second Person, and the Holy Spirit is the one sent with the message.

If we take the story of Jesus' walking the earth from the start of his life to the finish in the way the New Testament interprets that story, then in the baptism of Jesus we have a picture of the Trinity taking to its embrace fallen human nature, uniting us sinners with Jesus in what is now unconditional forgiveness as well as unconditional love. The Holy Spirit extends an olive branch to all human beings, saying in effect that the flood of God's anger is over, if indeed it ever existed except in our own guilty fears.

However, in the story of the transfiguration of Jesus on the mountain the Trinity is depicted as doing something different, something that takes matters further than the baptism left them.

Jesus is there, seen transfigured in a heavenly light, a light beyond the power of any human dyer to create. The Father is present as the first speaker, not now saying to Jesus, 'You are my beloved Son', but saying to Peter, James and John, 'This is my beloved Son, in whom I am well pleased. Listen to him.' Jesus is appointed the second speaker, who is to be listened to. And in place of the dove, we have a cloud indicating the presence of the Holy Spirit. This is not an ordinary cloud, since we are told the voice of the Father speaks from out of the cloud. The end result of the mysterious incident is that Jesus is to be listened to. Jesus is the audible reflection of the Father's love and forgiveness.

In other words, when we listen to Jesus we hear the voice of the Father reflected in our own world. We have in our ears not just what someone thinks God is saying, but the words of someone who experiences God's love, who as the Lamb knows what it is to be loved by the Great Shepherd, and who then makes it known to us. What we are to hear from Jesus comes to us by the second 'procession', it proceeds from the mouth of Jesus but is a completely true reflection of the love that the First Person first gave him. In words and in example it is Love-in-return-for-love.

I suggested above in Chapter Three that anyone may revisit the story of the baptism of Jesus as if Jesus had come up out of the water and said to my reader, 'You next!' The heart of what is involved in being baptized is there in a gospel image. A further suggestion may be made regarding the transfiguration: we may imagine ourselves going up the mountain with Jesus and Peter and James and John; to see what happens to Jesus and how the disciples react; then to be asked by Jesus to stand where he stood, and have the Trinity embrace us in a way different from the baptism. Here on the mountain standing with Jesus I am still and always the beloved son or daughter in whom God is well pleased for reasons known only to God's love. The Father's voice says my name, repeats his words of adoption, and tells the world they must listen to me.

Thus I am called to witness. Thus I need the power of Jesus, the second 'procession' of the Holy Spirit, to give me the strength to do the impossible. In essence, the call is very simple: to tell the world that I, a sinner, am none the less a son or daughter of God by God's own choosing, a privilege which is open to anyone who is willing to believe in it. That after all is the essence of what Jesus did after the transfiguration: he went to face the religious authorities in Jerusalem, and when they asked him, 'Are you the Christ, the Son of the Blessed One?' he said 'Yes, I am.' So they had him killed as a blasphemer. That reminds us how earnestly Jesus, even Jesus, prayed before this confrontation, and how we need to pray earnestly ahead of being mocked or tested for our belief.

Not every Christian denomination celebrates Confirmation as a sacrament, but all Christians have some form of saying thank you to God by lives of faithful service. The Sacrament of Confirmation is an ideal way of recreating the movement of the Gospels in our own lives. I remember as a teenager asking why we had to receive the Holy Spirit in Confirmation when we had already received the same Spirit in Baptism. Going back to Jesus' baptism and transfiguration as models provides the perfect answer. In my baptism the Holy Spirit came to me and stayed contentedly still; in my confirmation the Holy Spirit bounces me back to God not just in love but in love and service.

The origin of those words of the Father, 'Listen to him', lies deep in a prophesy found in the Old Testament. When Moses lay dying, his closest companions were dismayed at the thought of losing their leader, and of losing him before they had reached the Promised Land. Then, depending on which account we read, either God told them not to be afraid (Dt 18:18), or Moses himself told them not to be afraid (Dt 18:15), because God would raise up another prophet like Moses who would complete the work. And, 'To him they will listen'. At first it seemed that Joshua was the one prophesied, but Joshua died and the work was still not finished. More than a thousand years later, in the time of Jesus, 'the Prophet' was still awaited. The Promised Land was still occupied by a foreign force, the kingdom of God was not yet a reality on earth, so who and where was 'the Prophet'? (John 7:40)

The Apostle Peter recognized (Acts 3:22,23) that Jesus was the one: after the pattern of Moses, Jesus was leading the human race from slavery, into the freedom of knowing God's love and forgiveness, giving them a completely new reason for living a good life, opening the gates of a new land where unconditional love and forgiveness are the rule. But this is a divine world, and we cannot find the way back to God by our own human strength, unless it be by a gift from Jesus. The lambs will be safe, as long as those called to be shepherds rely on the Spirit of Jesus, and not on their own spirit.

So it seems that the two processions of the Holy Spirit, from the Father and from the Son, may be traced in the two big visions of Jesus described by Mark and Matthew and Luke. And they are reflected in the Christian rites of initiation to this day.

Another place where we might see the two processions working separately but in tandem is in the standard shape of the prayers of the Eucharist. I say 'in tandem' because once again they come in the right order, from the First Person first then from the Second Person. The first invocation of the Holy Spirit comes, in nearly every Eucharistic Prayer ever written, before the consecration of the bread and wine. We ask of the Father, or the presiding priest asks on our behalf, that the Spirit will come down upon these gifts of bread and wine, so that they may become, or become for us, the body and blood of Christ. The words of consecration will state, over the bread, 'This is my body', and over the wine, 'This is my blood'; the Holy Spirit, the spirit of truth, will bring the gift from God to help us believe the words. They will be true; through the Spirit they will become true for us who hear them. That communication is a gift from the Father, the First Person.

After the consecration, in nearly every version of the Eucharistic Prayer ever written, there is a second invocation of the Holy Spirit. The prayer asks that we who receive the body and blood of Christ may become one body, one spirit in Christ, along with believers everywhere, and unbelievers as well, and the saints and all the living and the dead, so as to give glory all together one day through Christ, with him and in him, and that unity will be the unity of the Holy Spirit. We could say, the words of consecration are extended to cover the whole Church and ultimately the whole world and the human race. We are all to be the one body of Christ, we are all to be one spirit, the blood of Christ.

Now this second invocation of the Holy Spirit is 'work in progress', whereas the first invocation was accomplished there and then. The words of consecration are effective when they are said, but the second invocation is for the work of Jesus from now till the end of the world, to make the world one body, one spirit in Christ. The second invocation has to do with the right hand side of the diagram I drew above; it has to do with our response in love to the love of the First Person, and we can only respond in the Spirit of Jesus, namely in the Holy Spirit as sent by Jesus in the second 'procession'.

Prayer to be transfigured: Lord Jesus, we ask you to give us the second gift, to share your courage and faithfulness. We want to thank your Father for his adoption of us as his children, a gift beyond our wildest dreams. Already we can tell him how peaceful that knowledge makes us, but we know our own weakness: we try to put our thanks into deeds, and all too often we get distracted or tempted away from what we know your Father would want us to do. So now we ask for a share in your spirit, in the Holy Spirit as that Spirit finds its way back to the Father. We want our message to the One to be absolutely clear, as his message to us is quite clear. As you, even you, prayed for strength hour after hour before your trial, so we pray for strength to be wholehearted. And if we fail yet again, we pray for the good sense to return to you and try again. We are human, and we ask for your strength which is divine. Amen.

7

'Them bones ...'

'Them bones, them bones, them dry bones ...' So runs the refrain of the famous spiritual song. The bones in question are to be found in Chapter Thirty-Seven of the book of Ezekiel in the Bible. Ezekiel in his vision is taken to a valley covered all over with dry bones, bones of dead people from Israel's past. He is asked by his visionary guide whether the bones will come back to life again, and Ezekiel is at first pretty sure, as anyone would be, that very dry bones are well past the possibility of ever being part of a living being again. But he says to his guide, 'You know better than I do'. Then the Lord God tells Ezekiel to prophesy over the bones, and tell them to come to life again.

So Ezekiel speaks out over the valley, and tells the bones to sort themselves out, and to come together as separate creatures, and to take on sinews and flesh, then to be covered over by skin. Lo and behold, with a great rattling till the operation is over, the bones do come together to skeletons, sinews appear, and flesh, and skin covers all. Then Ezekiel is told to summon the winds from north, south, east and west, to come and enter the restored beings and give them breath and life. Which he does, and the winds come, and the creatures breathe again, against every human expectation.

The prophet understood the vision to mean that the people of Israel would be brought together again as a people, with their own land and their own temple and their own dwellings. At the time they were scattered, having been blitzed by the Babylonian army and suffering all their important leaders and citizens being led into exile. The temple of Solomon was a ruin, the nation was in ruins. Could it ever be restored again? The campaign of the Babylonian army was designed to stop that ever happening again: theirs was a scorched-earth policy of conquest.

Eventually, some seventy years after the scattering of the people, they were able to re-unite as a nation, an event as unlikely as the dance of the bones, no longer dry. Babylon was conquered by the Persian king Cyrus, whose policy was the exact opposite of scorched-earth. Cyrus believed that he had no chance of success with a huge empire unless he respected the religions and customs of the subject nations. Accordingly he issued an edict known as the Cyrus Cylinder, a copy of which may still be seen in the British Museum today, decreeing that the nations exiled to Babylon should be allowed to return with their sacred articles of worship to where they came from, and to rebuild their own cities. The miraculous thing Ezekiel saw happen in his vision of the dry bones came to pass: the people of Jerusalem in exile were allowed and even encouraged to go home to Jerusalem, rebuild the walls, rebuild the temple, and live there again.

I amused myself one time when planning to talk about Ezekiel and the dry bones. I created a small valley of dry cocktail sticks and took a transparency photo of the sad little pile. Then I began to build up a picture of a stork standing on one leg, stick by cocktail stick, taking a photo each time another stick was added. Eventually I had a series of a dozen or more pictures, moving from the sad small pile to an upstanding bird skeleton. Then I added on a photo from nature, of a stork standing fishing; then finally a picture of a stork flying happily away. It was all just a primitive visual aid, but surprisingly effective, as the viewers of the sequence saw a bundle of sticks gradually click into place and get skin, feathers and flight. Of course it depended on the fact that I knew from the outset where I was going.

All of that is what the Holy Spirit does. The scattered members of a community large or small, the whole human race or the smallest family, are gathered together by the Holy Spirit in love and forgiveness. Even within a single human being, the Spirit is at work integrating the human spirit as this one child of the one God of love. Every time our balance gets disturbed, and we begin to totter towards depression or over-elation, the Spirit is inviting us gently or firmly back into the centre of ourselves, half-way between nothing and God, as this child of God. Each of us has a centre point, a point of balance, and the Spirit helps us lean down if we are too high, and lean upwards if we are too down. Evil and harm can usually be traced back to our acting vigorously when we are off balance, thus upsetting those around us and unbalancing them as well as ourselves.

When we are very low in spirits, we tend to cast a gloom on all around us; the Spirit on the other hand is reminding us quietly all the time that we are precious to God. Whichever of the two thoughts we feed, that will determine whether we get better or grow worse. When we are at peace with ourselves, then we are at our most creative and co-operative. When we are high because over-anxious, then again we cause trouble, taking too much on ourselves and thinking we might lose the esteem of God and of everyone else if our current project fails. If we are high and thinking our work is a work of sublime art, we can lose touch with reality and confuse all around us. The Holy Spirit guides us all the time towards the centre of our moods, away from the scattering effects of extremes of mood.

I am a firm believer that evil is something we create ourselves, not a cruel force or spiritual being attacking us from outside. I described already the parable of Laurel and Hardy and the Christmas trees. The Holy Spirit is the integrating spirit, and we are vulnerable, oftentimes wayward, beings who aim too high and then get depressed when we fail to reach our goals. The Spirit is the one who reminds us that we are not rubbish, since we are God's children; on the other hand we are not God, but only God's children.

There is as much scattering of the human race going on as there has ever been in the history of the world. Whole nations are displaced, and are either striving to get back to the lands from which they were ousted, or else trying desperately to be adopted as members of another nation. One of my friends, who has been intimately involved in the refugee service, notes a surprising fact: in the refugee camps, as much is achieved by the refugees themselves clubbing together in mutual help, as is done by the supervising refugee services. The Holy Spirit is at work from within, creating unities which were not planned by the planners from outside.

When we reach rock bottom in our lives, then it can happen that we find the ultimate low is indeed rock, the rock of God's love which has never deserted us in spite of appearances. Human history is full of stories of men, women and children who have refused to take 'No' for an answer and who have begun building up their lives each and every time they were knocked down. I am reminded of the way a huge chestnut tree fell apart one hot summer here in the grounds of the retreat house where I live. The chestnut tree had to be cut up and carted away, but within a year or two there were a dozen small trees growing in the space, and wild flowers that had been unable to see the light before. Nature does not seem to know the meaning of the word Despair. Nor does the Holy Spirit.

Prayer: Heavenly Father, in the beginning your Spirit brooded over the whole world. From chaos came order, and life, and beauty. Yet there is in us human beings a wayward leaning to left and right of the way you point out to us. We think we can see more clearly than the obvious, the humdrum. We sail off into uncharted waters, and find we have ended up in a land of nonsense and quarrels and greed. Please send the same Spirit who brought order and beauty out of chaos, and work the miracle of creation all over again. 'Reclothe us in our rightful mind', as the hymn asks of you. To be loved is all we really need, but to know that we are loved; then we become a whole person.

Lord Jesus, Saviour, you it is who send the Spirit of re-creation. Your Father sends the Spirit and lifts us off the ground; you send the Spirit and keep us firmly fixed in reality, ready for hard work in your company, till order and beauty are restored. Once I have become this one person, loved and appreciated by your Father, then I can respond to your call to make the rest of the world one, starting with where I find myself. Make me a channel of your love. You yourself compared your own expected death and resurrection to the history of the time when the temple was destroyed but surprisingly rebuilt. May we always live for the resurrection in our own lives. May we refuse to take the 'No' of misfortune for an answer, but always look to your grace to put us back together again, and in a way better than the way we were before. Amen.

8

Plotting a Route

The Holy Spirit watches over our route through life like a guardian angel. If we wish, we may think of guardian angels, but I prefer to think of the Holy Spirit taking a personal interest in each of our journeys. When we are on the right course, there is what we might call a 'feel-good factor' about what we are doing. The spiritual writers call it 'consolation'. This 'feeling good' does not always mean the same as feeling comfortable. I would say that even Jesus in his agony in the garden just before his arrest could be said to have the feel-good factor: he knew, after praying so long and so hard, that the way forward in his Father's eyes was to stay and face the consequences of his life's choices, even though that meant facing a terrible death. There are times in anyone's life when we can only feel good about feeling uncomfortable: the only way forward is through the darkened valley.

This 'consolation' comes of doing things that integrate our lives, integrate rather than scatter. Its opposite, normally called 'desolation', scatters our forces, moves our lives in the direction of the dry bones such as Ezekiel saw in his vision. I will give some examples of consolation and desolation in the next chapter, but for the moment it will be good to get an overall picture of how we grow with the Holy Spirit, and how we go astray when we ignore the Spirit. I may safely take it that anyone who has picked up this book and read this far is a person of good will. The encouraging thoughts that come to someone like that will be coming from the Holy Spirit, whereas any thought or feelings that leave such a person desolate and discouraged will not be from the Holy Spirit.

If not from the Holy Spirit, then from where? We do not have to speculate that there are beings called evil spirits waiting around to trip us up; that to me would be an intolerable way of going through life, and a plain contradiction of God's providence and the gift of the Holy Spirit. What happens is, through inattention we wander from the straight way forward, and find ourselves like someone in a forest who has wandered from the path. Without the clear track in front, all the trees look much the same, and we are just as likely to end in a ditch as to find the path again. Or, we are like sailors on a small boat who do not keep a watch on the sea-tides and so get swept into difficulties. In human terms, when we find ourselves in desolation, we are just as likely to make bad choices as good ones, flailing around trying to get out of a situation with no clear exit.

Attention, therefore, is the key. Outside my window I can watch small birds feeding on a basket of nuts: they have to work to get at each peanut, but nearly every second they lift and turn their heads to see if any rival is approaching, to see if any sparrow hawk is swooping, to see if they are in any danger at all. They do not know the luxury most humans enjoy, of going about their business unafraid, not constantly on the alert and expecting serious trouble. Yet did not Jesus time and again warn his disciples, as they came towards Jerusalem and the climax of his life, to 'Watch and pray', and to 'Take heed'? St Mark's Gospel has Jesus saying the one or the other eight times in just two chapters. 'What I say to you I say to all, "Watch!"' (Mark 13:37) St Ignatius of Loyola tells anyone in desolation to go back to what they decided when they were clear, when the way ahead was clear, and the sooner we do that the lesser the danger of getting thoroughly lost.

Temptations, therefore, are best regarded not as some evil character trying to get us to turn our backs on our good resolutions, but rather as our own human weakness, unsure whether we can keep going on the straight path. Some temptations are clearly temptations, nothing but, and once we get going in God's ways the blatant temptations become less tempting, when we have enjoyed the peace of living in God's way. What then happens is that the temptations become more subtle, as we begin to think we can never be fooled again. We have to learn that not every good idea that occurs to us comes necessarily from God. St Ignatius, and his favourite author Thomas à Kempis (writer of the classic *On the Imitation of Christ*) both tell us to test every seemingly good idea, to follow it through to its consequences and see where it is likely to lead: whether to something completely good, or ultimately to stress and confusion, 'too much of a good thing'.

Even St Paul the Apostle, though his vision of the risen Jesus was completely true and from God, mistakenly thought he had to get up and preach Jesus right away to the followers of Jesus he came a few days previously to arrest and imprison for believing in Jesus. They were not amused, they were bemused; Paul had to leave town, go away into the desert and re-think his theology. Likewise any of us, if we find a bright idea that seemed to come from God has led us in the end into serious confusion of heart, we need to look back, note where we got it wrong, and be prepared to avoid the same trap another time.

The temptations that are obviously temptations usually hit us when we are low and desolate. The subtle temptations usually slip in when we are 'high', and feeling as if we can do no wrong, that we will surely never make a mistake again. Ignatius tells us that now and then, not to everyone, not always, God can and may 'speak' to a heart completely unexpectedly, out of the blue and against all the odds. The way Jesus appeared to the disciples after his resurrection lifted them from near despair to deep joy in a moment. Even then they wisely waited around to know what God wanted them to do about it, until at the feast of Pentecost it became clear.

The Holy Spirit given to us enables us to say, to cry, 'Abba!' 'Father!' to God, any time, any where, before temptation, in temptation, after temptation whether we were successful or whether we failed to resist. This is the way St Paul tells us to use, following the example of Jesus in his agony in the garden of Gethsemane, to climb back into the arms of God as a well-loved child. What then of the frightening saying of Jesus about the Sin against the Holy Spirit which 'can never be forgiven'? The simplest answer is to understand that it can never be forgiven as long as we are ensnared in it, but it can be forgiven as soon as we stop doing it. And 'Abba!' is the clue. To sin against the Holy Spirit is to refuse forgiveness, either because like the Pharisees we think we are perfect already, or because, like the Prodigal Son amongst the pigs, we have not yet remembered the depth of love our Abba has for us. God is at a loss to convey forgiveness through the Holy Spirit to those who will not accept it. But if a Pharisee comes to his senses (like Paul), or a sinner decides to trust in God's forgiveness, there is no longer any sin against the Holy Spirit, and the forgiveness which was always there can get through.

Prayer: *Holy Spirit, stabilizer of our lives, be with us all along our journey through life, just as, in the Bible story of Tobias, the Archangel Raphael watched over every step of the journey, keeping Tobias from harm. When we are troubled by temptations to give up living a good life, show us small steps that we could well manage, teach us to live just one day at a time. When all is well, keep us alert like the little birds feeding, so as not to be taken by surprise. 'Just because a thing is simple, that doesn't mean it is easy', as the saying goes. And when we are on top of the world and think our troubles are all in the past, teach us to examine each and every good idea to see where it is likely to land us.*

And wherever we are in our state of mind and heart, teach us to cry 'Abba!' to God, and never, never to doubt that our Abba hears us with a loving and forgiving ear. Amen.

9

Telling True from False

In this chapter I wish simply to give some examples from the life of St Ignatius of Loyola and also from my own life, of how false steps can be turned into the true way, by the providence of God. The sensation in our hearts as we finally get back onto the right path is one place where we especially feel the presence of the Holy Spirit.

Ignatius was a late starter in the spiritual life. From being a courtier and a part-time soldier he was reduced to a long spell of convalescence with nothing to do but dream. His knee and his former dreams were both shattered by an enemy cannon ball. His new dreams were all to do with following Christ wholeheartedly, wherever that might take him. Over the following months he was blessed with understanding and insights into how to lead others to Christ in ways like the way he himself was led. He started putting together his little book of *Spiritual Exercises* which is still invaluable five hundred years later.

As I mentioned above in Chapter Two, the trouble was that Ignatius was a layman with the wrong kind of reputation, and heresy-hunters were soon after him. Who was he, to be teaching the faithful with no visible religious qualifications for doing so? After a couple of spells in prison as guest of the Inquisition, Ignatius determined to get the acceptable qualifications, no matter what it cost. He went back to school at the age of thirty, to learn Latin, the language spoken in the universities. Then to university in Spain for philosophy, in Paris for theology, begging his way to obtain the tuition fees. It was while he was studying theology that he fell prey to a temptation of interest to our present chapter. It seemed like a good idea at the time, but it could have wrecked his hopes of qualification.

The lectures in theology fired his heart and mind so much that he could not wait to go home to his lodgings and pray for hours the beauty of the truths he was hearing. In his own way, in his own heart, he knew most of them already, but to find himself in the mainstream of the age-long mysteries of God was sheer bliss, and he prayed daily into the small hours of the night. The trouble was, of course, that he was soon becoming unfit to attend properly to the next day's lectures and tasks. Reluctantly at first, he got himself to bed at a proper time, now that he realized that to carry on the long prayer times was an indulgence and could destroy his chances of getting a degree and being ordained priest. His long labour of learning Latin and Philosophy would have been wasted, and he would still not be allowed to teach his *Spiritual Exercises* without being harassed by the Inquisitors.

So, his lovely prayer times were in fact leading him up the wrong path, when it came to his main desire in life. They were attractive, they seemed good at the time, but they were a snare. Once he was back on track, he realized with relief that he had been guided by the Holy Spirit to return to his main purpose.

Earlier still in Ignatius' new spiritual life he had turned very scrupulous, wanting to tell in confession to one priest after another every last detail of the things he now saw as wrong in his previous thirty years of life. This time the spiral was downwards into depression, rather than upwards into ecstasy: he was tempted to throw himself down a well that yawned invitingly outside his window and end it all, rather than endure the torment of forever remembering something else and wondering if he had confessed it properly. Instead, by the grace of God, he came to his senses and saw that such scruples could not be from the Holy Spirit since they were completely negative and soul-destroying. To put it in the prophet Ezekiel's terms, the scruples were moving him in the direction of the dry bones, rather than in the direction of a vibrant life with which to praise God.

Such upsets and recoveries of good sense can happen in much more humdrum lives. In my own life there have been several, more than the average number because of a bi-polar condition that tends to push me to extremes of feeling: over-excitement or over-depression, both of which are forms of desolation. Consolation is found in the stable centre, not in the extremes. For example, in my time as a student of philosophy I once made myself ill. I got so wrapped up in writing an essay that I could not stop for an entire week, the while getting more and more confused instead of clearer about the subject of the essay. Again later on in life, over many years, playing the guitar and singing folk songs as an entertainer was a pleasant hobby of mine, but I ended up with a repertoire of over 300 songs to keep up and many people and places expecting entertainment from me, and the whole thing began to be a burden instead of a help. Another skill I had was the taking of a good photograph: I have an eye for a good picture. Where that managed to become a burden was because I noted every single negative over thirty years, thousands of them, just so that I could get copies if I or anyone else wanted a copy of a particular shot. Luckily that has been hit on the head by the arrival of digital cameras, so I have quietly bowed out of the photography business and left it to the younger generations.

These may seem trivial examples, and nothing to do with the spiritual life, but these are the sorts of dilemmas we get ourselves into, starting something with enthusiasm and then finding we cannot stand the pace, and they can colour the rest of life and damage the greater good, and that is of concern to the Holy Spirit.

On a more obviously spiritual level, there were two ambitions which seemed to be given the green light in the life of a Jesuit, by Father George Walkerley, my novice master in my first two years as a young Jesuit: it was all right for a Jesuit to be a writer, and it was all right to have a desire to be a future novice master if asked. The writing has never been a trouble: I find it easier to have a book in preparation than to have nothing to write, and it has never given me anything but peace of heart in the past fifty years. But I did dream of myself as a future novice master, and was so astonished when the Provincial asked me to prepare for the role that I neglected to recognize the telltale signs of over-excitement. My life as novice master lasted just two months, and my breakdown caused serious trouble for a whole number of people. Not every seemingly good idea comes from God.

To get back to Ignatius. Later on in his life someone asked him how long it would take him to be reconciled in his heart, if the Pope decided to disband the Society of Jesus. By this time Ignatius felt that his life's story had finally ended up in the right place, with nearly a thousand men already working as Jesuits in every continent of the world, taking the ideals of the *Spiritual Exercises* with them. How long, then, would it take him to be reconciled? Incredibly, he reckoned 'a quarter of an hour.' Perhaps five minutes to plummet in dismay, then ten minutes to say to himself, 'I only started this for the greater glory of God. If God no longer wants it, then as always I will try to find out what God wants instead.' Peace of heart comes from doing what God wants, not what I want.

I remember being taught about 'inspiration' by one Father Kevin Smythe who was on the teaching staff when I first studied theology. He was talking specifically about the books of the Bible, and he maintained that we believe in the inspiration of the biblical books with certainty because the tradition of the Church has singled them out as being inspired by the Holy Spirit when their authors put them together. But, said Kevin, that is not to say that lots of other books are not equally inspired. The only difference could be that the Church has never certified them as inspired. Inspiration is not something that only happens when the Church solemnly declares it to be happening.

That same truth could be applied to the matter of this chapter. All sorts of choices in our lives, whether or not they appear to have anything to do with religion, could just the same be where the Holy Spirit is operating. The Spirit leads us, sometimes by roundabout ways, to what God wanted of us all the time, but it sometimes takes us ages to find again the way of peace.

Prayer to arrive at full circle: Holy Trinity of God, keep me within your embrace. Father, it is you who call me from up ahead. Jesus Son of God, it is you who accompany me as I head for home. Holy Spirit, it is you who keep me poised between Father and Son, between the First and Second Persons, on the true road. From small stories as well as from great in my past life, teach me to know ever more quickly your presence, Holy Spirit. Great is the relief when I have seen the silliness of my ways and thrown off burdens that were of my own making. Give me wisdom to sense your presence early on, and to stay close to the way you are indicating as best for me. Let me be satisfied with what is enough for me, instead of rambling for years in search of false goals. Amen.

10

No Exercise for Pentecost?

What was so special about *The Spiritual Exercises*, the little book Ignatius took such pains to see published with the blessing of the Church? It was, and is, a summary of the way God worked with Ignatius in the months following his conversion to a thoughtful, prayerful apostolic life. Not only does it outline the steps, but it invites the one doing the exercises to pray intensely for thirty days, following the divine logic Ignatius had been taught. Really the book of the *Exercises* is not a book for reading at all, but a tool to carry on a living tradition. Ignatius himself led many friends and followers through his exercises, and some at least of those who had been through them with him were able, by means of the guidebook, to lead others in the same paths, since the guidebook is essentially a guide for the leader, and is only intended at second hand for the one being guided.

The actual Exercises for the retreatant to follow are divided up into four weeks. The first week is the groundwork, helping the one making the Exercises to see himself or herself as a sinner, but a sinner still loved by God. Out of that comes not grovelling before God, but instead a huge sense of gratitude, that in spite of all I have done and all I have failed to do, I am still here and still loved by God. Simple gratitude is enough, and Ignatius does not expect the majority of his listeners to go further; but for those who are really fired up with gratitude and who wish to make a more generous return to God, Ignatius goes on to the second, third and fourth weeks of Exercises. These involve praying four or five hours a day immersed in the gospel story of the life of Christ, starting with his infancy and childhood, then his public life and preaching, then Holy Week and his Passion, then finally his Resurrection. He leads the one praying through all the resurrection appearances of Jesus mentioned in the Gospels and the Acts of the Apostles, but stops with the Ascension of Christ into heaven. He does not feature the descent of the Holy Spirit as the climax of the sequence.

What does Ignatius put there instead? As one brought up on the *Spiritual Exercises*, how do I hold on to the Holy Spirit as the central force of the whole process, if the story for Ignatius seems to stop short of the sending of the Holy Spirit by Christ from the Father as Jesus promised?

What Ignatius puts as the finale of the Exercises is what he calls a Contemplation to obtain the love of God. As a preliminary he says that love is shown in sharing, and that love is shown in deeds more than in words. Then the points to be contemplated are: first, how many gifts God has given me, gifts of creation, gifts of rescue and personal gifts not given to anyone else; then to see the invitation to give in return, all that I have and am. Second, to contemplate how God dwells in me and wants to be there; then how I am invited to dwell in God my lover. Third, how God labours for me, has laboured from the beginning of time for me; and how it is only fitting to do more than a little work for God. Fourthly, to be aware that God is 'in all things and above all things' (as the prayer of the Church puts it), that everything I touch or see comes from God to me like sunbeams from the sun or like a stream from its source; so might I in turn find God in everything.

Why I have always felt quite at home with the finale of the *Spiritual Exercises* in spite of all I believe about the Holy Spirit, is because the two fit perfectly together. What Ignatius is putting before us to contemplate is really none other than the two Processions of the Holy Spirit. God the First Person loves, unconditionally, and the Holy Spirit thus proceeds in our direction. The risen Jesus receives the love, with us and for us, and urges us to share in the return of love. By ourselves, like the Apostles and disciples, we are unable to withstand persecution until Jesus is risen and has returned to his Father. Now the time has come, and we can share in the second Procession, giving back love to the First Person in the power of Christ who is the Second Person.

Thus the big divide in the Exercises between the first week and the remaining three weeks corresponds to the divide between the Holy Spirit proceeding from the First Person and the same Holy Spirit proceeding from the Second Person. Implicit too is the notion of 'justification by faith', since a person of good will, having completed the first week as a forgiven sinner, is already justified by faith, but there is further to go for those who hear and answer the call, to go from love and gratitude in truth but in words, to love and gratitude in action in imitation of Jesus. Even as early as Ignatius of Antioch (d. 107), from whom Inigo Loyola took his official Latin name, we find that martyr writing, 'Faith is the beginning, love is the end, and the union of both together is God.' (Ignatius, *To the Ephesians* 14)

What Ignatius Loyola is fostering in his Exercises is first of all a basic willingness to be loved and forgiven by God, with a determination to try to do good and avoid evil for the future; but then his desire is to awaken a zeal and earnest desire to go further, to be a genuine disciple, to do outstanding things in life to foster love of Jesus and of what Jesus stands for. This double aim of Ignatius seems to me to correspond to the two levels that appear in the Gospels. Jesus did not say, 'If you want to be saved, take up your cross and follow me', but he did say, 'If you want to be my disciple, take up your cross and follow me'. There were thousands of ordinary people in the life of Jesus who were not disciples, but whom he healed and fed and taught none the less. The disciples were to be the leaven in the mass. They were to be shepherds of the sheep, the light to show the way, the fishers to catch the fish.

So the four points of the Contemplation, about God's gifts to me, God's presence in me, God's work for me and God's presence in everything for me, are all implicit from the beginning of the Exercises, but now near the end of thirty days of prayer they can be seen as a loving invitation: God saying, 'I have done all this for you, can you not love me back as I have loved you?' This is New Testament wisdom, infinitely beyond the commandments given to Moses. Those said, 'You must love the Lord your God . . .' Here, following Jesus, Ignatius gives a wealth of reasons why to love God, reasons which all add up to 'God has loved you first; and how God has loved you!' In the nature of things, no one can order another person to 'Love me with all your heart!' Anyone who wants to be loved needs first of all to show love, and then to wait for a free response. Ignatius accordingly does not, even after thirty days, say 'You must', but only 'Surely anyone with any feelings at all would respond, in all reason and justice; surely you ought to make your response even if you are tired after all this praying and all these exercises, as one making a gift with heartfelt love?'

This may be the place to have a look at the one saying attributed to Jesus which is not in the Gospels, namely, 'It is more blessed to give than to receive.' (Acts 20:35) The saying comes at the end of St Paul's farewell speech to the elders of the church of Ephesus, as he reminds them to have a care for the weak ones of this world, quoting words that he says come from Jesus. How does all I have been saying about the two Processions of the Holy Spirit square up with that saying of Jesus?

I think this may be related to the way Jesus says, in the discourse at the Last Supper, 'The Father is greater than I.' (John 14:28) The most obvious way that statement is true lies in the fact that God the First Person, the Father, loves without having been first loved by another, whereas Jesus as Son of God is first loved and then loves in return for love. Totally uncaused, unconditional love is by its nature 'greater' than love given in return for love.

I think it all depends what we mean by 'more blessed'. To be loved by God as God's child, freely, is a gift beyond compare, and the foundation of all love and of all life. There is no greater gift. All the same, when inspired by God's love for us we manage with the Holy Spirit to give unconditional love ourselves to another person, then that is greater than simply being loved. We are, in the strength of Christ, behaving in imitation of the way God behaves, loving but asking nothing in return. So we find for instance in Luke's Gospel, 'When you give a party, do not invite those who will ask you back, but ask those who will not be able to ask you back, the poor, the maimed, the blind, the lame. Do that, and you will be blessed.'

(Luke 14:12-14) To receive God's love is the happiest of gifts, but then to be able to walk in our Father's footsteps and do as God does is a divine blessing even though it may involve difficulty and heartbreak.

Prayer: Heavenly Father, First Person God, there is no gift greater than the gift of your love for me. That you should adopt me as your own child, give me a place at your table, and take enormous steps to ensure I get there and will stay there, such love is all the difference to me. Either I am nothing, making a mess of my life and going nowhere, or I am secure as a prince in a royal household which will never crumble. I thank you with all my heart for the Spirit of adoption by which you are my very own 'Abba'.

It is one thing to be your child, your son or your daughter; it is another thing to be able to act as your son or as your daughter, loving what you love, giving what you give, working as you work, valuing what you value. For that we need your second gift, the gift of Jesus your Son and first-born, to be able to give you a return of divine love, divine gifts, divine work, divine values. We are humans, and do not possess the power to do divine things.

Lord Jesus, Friend and Brother, send from heaven the Holy Spirit as that Spirit proceeds from you, a spirit of gratitude that is not only grateful but effective in our poor world, to set the world to rights. Send to us, share with us, your Spirit to love our daily work and play. Send us your Spirit especially when things go wrong, when our enterprises come to nothing or to less than we had hoped; and even more especially when we are attacked by those who misunderstand our motives and who think religion, and particularly your religion, is a menace. 'To err is human; to forgive, divine.' Without you, Jesus, and the Spirit proceeding from you, we cannot do the divine thing. So for this we ask in your name. Amen.

11

Bread and Wine

When as a priest I am presiding at the Eucharist, there is something which often strikes me as it comes time for Communion. I stand in front of the altar, holding the paten with the consecrated hosts, while to either side of me stand the ministers each holding a chalice. What my role is stressing at that point, as I give each one the bread of life and say 'The body of Christ,' is to commemorate the death of Christ: here is Jesus who died for you. What then the chalice is stressing as the communicants come to take it, is the Resurrection of Christ. The words are, 'The blood of Christ' and the meaning: here is Jesus who rose for you. The words of consecration spoken earlier separated the body from the blood: body here, blood and water there, as it was on Calvary. Communion under both kinds brings together again in the communicants the body of Jesus, his human life and his divine life in a sacramental form, in each one who receives first the bread then the wine mixed with water.

Surely this is just like the shape of the Gospel of Mark, where the first half of the book is to do with healing and feeding, with bread and water, with no mention thus far of chalices, blood or death. Only when Peter has made his statement of faith about Jesus being the Christ, only then does Jesus turn to Jerusalem and his coming death in defence of what he believes in. What he believes in is his Abba's unconditional love and forgiveness, and he knows he will be killed for holding such a thing, but that his Abba will uphold him. When we receive Communion in the form of bread, there is no request that we go and die with Jesus, it is simply a gift of healing, feeding, and faith.

When on the other hand we approach the chalice, we are implicitly agreeing to live as disciples of Jesus, willing if need be to 'drink the cup that he drank.' The fact that it is a cup of wine indicates that the Spirit of Jesus will provide the intoxication to enable us to do for him things that the world calls madness. And so we come back to the two Processions of the Holy Spirit. Receiving the bread of the Eucharist, I am loved with no conditions by Jesus on behalf of his Father. I do not have to do anything except say 'Thank you', and I will still be loved just the same if I forget to say 'Thank you'. Receiving the chalice, I am relying on the love Jesus has for his Father, and asking for the same gift for myself. Receiving the bread I am a lamb; receiving the chalice I am risking to become a shepherd. Given the body of Christ I believe; given the blood of Christ I love.

Lest anyone think I am making all this up out of my own head without any backing from tradition, I would like to quote again Ignatius of Antioch. '. . . take a fresh grip on your faith (the very flesh of the Lord) and your love (the life-blood of Jesus Christ).' (*To the Trallians* 8) Or again, 'There is no pleasure for me in any meats that perish, or in the delights of this life; my desire is for the bread of God, even the flesh of Jesus Christ, who is the seed of David; and for my drink I crave that blood of his which is love imperishable.' (*To the Romans* 7) Not quite so clearly, yet again Ignatius writes, 'I have seen how immovably settled in faith you are; nailed body and soul as it were to the cross of the Lord Jesus Christ, and rooted and grounded in love by his blood.' (*To the Philadelphians* 1)

The Father loved the Son from all eternity, and the Son from before all time loved in return for love. In our world, the Son took it on himself to tell the world about God's love and forgiveness, and was killed for daring to do so. Through his death and Resurrection, the truth about God's loving nature came through to those who could hear, and it was the Holy Spirit who carried the love through from Father to Son to us. For the Son it was easy (so to speak) to be loved from all eternity; but to love in return by risking everything so as to tell us the news we had failed to grasp, that was anything but easy. Then in turn it happens for those who hear Jesus, when the news penetrates our heads and hearts what God is really like, that is nothing but joy; when however we try to tell the world around us, and to demonstrate the same in our actions, that is not easy.

The easy part is given as a gift by God, and we do not have to pray for it, but simply to accept it. We are sheep in God's pasture, we are adopted children, God's light is there for us, we are little fish caught in his net, we are coins with his image upon us, we are little children, we are not lost but found, we are on a sure foundation, we are forgiven. If however we wish to return the love, it means becoming as well all the active forms of the blessing for others: from sheep to shepherd, from adopted children to servants, from enlightened to becoming lights for others, from caught fish to fishers, from coins to treasure hunters, from children to beings with power, from being lost to showing the way, from sitting safe on rock to being a rock for others, from being forgiven to forgiving all others.

Just as surely as a lamb cannot become a shepherd by its own power, so surely we have to pray for this second Procession of the Holy Spirit to flow through us. Even the Lamb of God himself had to pray long and earnestly for the power to speak up on trial for who he truly was. Peter on the other hand, who had failed to pray when invited, more or less disintegrated when he was in the courtyard of the high priest, because he had not yet received the Spirit who was to be sent by Jesus. The second gift of the Spirit is to be able to call God my own 'Abba' when under persecution or severe hardship, to acknowledge the love and forgiveness of God in action and in deed. Thus, there is faith, and there is love. There is one Body, and one Spirit. (Ephesians 4:4) The wine, being intoxicating, tells us again that we cannot do great things for love of God, without the ingredient to turn us from water into wine.

I have a young friend who has his own band and sings thoughtful songs of his own creation. I was agreeably surprised to hear him singing, not about himself,

I am the left hand of God,
and I'm much harder to understand.
While the right hand will coddle you like a child,
I will push you to be a man.

Which is more or less what I have been saying, though not in
terms of left hand or right hand.[1]

There is a feeling among the faithful, often felt but lately
more often expressed, that the Holy Trinity has, at least in
name, a gender bias: two male-sounding titles and one gender-
less title. So, the argument goes, why not claim the Spirit for a
feminine title? The people who say this are in fact often encouraged by the way divine Wisdom in the Old Testament is
generally given a feminine image.

There is a double problem about this line of thought. First,
Old Testament Wisdom is not the same as the Holy Spirit, Third
Person of the Trinity; and, secondly, as far as New Testament
writers like St Paul are concerned, Jesus is the one who turns
out to be the Wisdom of God (1 Corinthians 1:24). So that
leaves us with the same problem we started with: how flexible
can we be, may we be, in attributing a 'he' or a 'she' or an 'it'
to the Holy Spirit? So, what did Jesus say?

As for Jesus himself, the Gospel of John has him sometimes
calling the Spirit 'it' since the Greek words for spirit, fire,
wind, water are neuter words. (e.g. John 14:17) But Jesus in
that Gospel also speaks of 'him'. For myself, and quite unof-
ficially, I think of the Holy Spirit as the divine personal 'It,
the spirit of love', which sometimes breathes like a gentle
father and sometimes like a vigorous mother wanting me to
'be a man'.

*Twofold prayer to the Holy Spirit: Now may I speak to you
yourself, Holy Spirit, 'Heavenly Dove' as you were named in the
hymn we sang yesterday. My Father, my Abba, might be in heaven
for all eternity loving me as his child, his lamb, his treasure and
all the rest, but if it was not for you I would never have heard the
blessed truth. Thank you for coming to me at my baptism, and
thank you for coming to my parents and godparents at their*

1 Mark Murphy, *St Peter and the Serpent*, CD Activate,
www.Wookiefoot.com

baptisms. And thank you then a thousand times for the thousand times you have brought home to me the reality of what was said and done at my baptism. You have whispered it to me, spoken it to me, shouted it to me, both by yourself and through the many, many men and women and children who have carried God's love in my direction. Whoever opened my eyes and my ears, and however it was done, I am eternally grateful.

On the other hand, 'How can I repay the Lord for his goodness to me? I will take the cup of salvation, I will call on the Lord's name.' (Psalm 116:12,13) My old friend Julian of Norwich called you 'God the Lord,'[2] and I call on your name through the power you gave to Jesus. I want to repay my Father for his unquestioning goodness, and I do not have the strength to do more than to say it in words or symbols. Put then your Spirit of intoxication into the chalice and into my life, to do what I cannot do. Make me a shepherd of the flock even while I am still God's lamb. If I stumble and fall, then let my stumbling and falling be my offering, but let me not stop trying to do great things for the One I love above all others. Amen.

---

2   See *Revelations of Divine Love*, Ch. 59, 'Our Father decides, our Mother works, our good Lord, the Holy Spirit, strengthens.'

12

Jesus Comes ...

This chapter and the next will be an illustrated way into the understanding of the Incarnation and the Redemption, by way of the symbols used in the Eucharist, namely bread, water and wine. Roughly speaking, the words used about the bread, water and wine in the preparation of the gifts recall the Incarnation, the coming of Christ into the world. The words and actions used at the consecration of the elements on the other hand recall our Redemption: his death for us; then the words and actions of Communion recall his rising to life, in himself and in us. The two Processions of the Holy Spirit are again seen in action, the first in the coming of Christ into the world, the second in the power of his sacrifice for us and the power he gives us to carry on his work.

A very useful framework to remember is the way St Paul speaks about body, soul and spirit. 'May the God of peace make you perfect and holy; and may you all be kept safe and blameless, spirit, soul and body, for the coming of our Lord Jesus Christ.' (1 Thessalonians 5:23) When I was a child being instructed in the catechism there was a foursome: Christ's body, blood, soul and divinity. Being four, after the theology of St Thomas Aquinas, it did not to my mind fit easily into the threefold materials of the Eucharist, namely the bread, the water and the wine. On the whole, I find it simpler all round to stay with St Paul and the theology of the time of Jesus. There is a beautiful simplicity in putting side by side the bread and the body, the water and the human life or soul, and the wine for the Spirit or the divinity. Christ had a human body, which was alive with human life, and a divine life full of the Spirit by which he called God his 'Abba'. The threefold division fits for Christ himself, for his brothers and sisters in the faith, and for the three elements of the Eucharist.

In the threefold division, what is meant by 'body' includes the blood, alive in a live body. Body is the physical presence of a living person, body is what you can touch, physically. 'Soul' in the language of Paul, is the life, the psyche, the intelligence, the element that answers back when you speak to a person, the element that moves a person to where that person wants to go. 'Spirit' as the third element is over and above ordinary life, and is something never experienced before in human history. Spirit for Paul is that which makes a follower of Jesus into a son or daughter of God, able to call God 'Abba' and able to call Jesus 'elder brother'. It is the spirit of adoption. (Galatians 4:6) This third element is divine, where the body and soul were human; but when the spirit is present, it pervades the body and the human life as well. We have a human being able and authorized to call God 'Abba'.

When the gifts are brought forward in the celebration of the Eucharist, the oldest tradition and the one still retained by Roman Catholics is to bring bread and a cup of wine mixed with water. The bread to represent the body of Christ presents no symbolic difficulty. For instance, in John's Gospel Jesus compares his body to the temple made by human hands, and bread was readily recognized as something human hands have made. 'Made by human hands' was a standard phrase for anything that is human as opposed to divine realities.

The water being mixed in with the wine is illuminated by the little centuries-old prayer used by Catholics: *By the mixing of this water and wine may we come to share in the divinity of Christ, who humbled himself to share in our human life.* An older version of the same prayer makes it clear that we are illustrating the Incarnation; the start of the prayer went like this: *O God who wonderfully created human nature and still more wonderfully re-created it; by the mixing . . .* etc. This prayer and this action is saying in symbols: Water is mixed with wine, human life is mixed with divine life. We are talking about the divine life of Christ with God from all eternity coming to dwell in a human body and life, such that Jesus fully human is the first in human history to call God 'Abba'. In technical language, the one Jesus has two natures, one human, the other divine.

Water into wine. We have the story of Jesus at the wedding feast of Cana to make it clear: wine stands for the divine element. The story as told by the evangelist makes it clear that Jesus is upgrading the water to wine. When it comes to weddings and celebrations, wine is better to have around than water, even though a world with wine only and no water would be fatal. In the story, Jesus is showing his power to raise human life to divine life – that is what the story means. So, water stands for human life, wine stands for divine life. This fits in with the meaning given to wine by the very early Christian writers: nowhere do they put wine in the category of things 'made by human hands'. Instead, they talk about wine as 'engendered by God', or as 'heavenly'. There is even a group of heretics condemned for using only bread and water in their Eucharist, because then how can they ever be raised to divine life?[1]

The reason why the reformers like Luther in the Protestant Reformation dropped the use of water from their reformed order of service for the Eucharist was over-sensitivity, in my own view. There was current a vague explanation of the water in the wine as meaning 'the human race', or 'the people'. So to speak, it goes, we have the body and blood of Christ, then here in the drop of water is our humble insignificant share in the work of Christ.[2] This explanation was even given to me as a child, so it is remarkable how shaky opinions can keep cropping up. Naturally and rightly Luther and the others would not allow 'us' to have any part in the salvation won for us long ago by Jesus and by nobody else but Jesus.

Where the reformers were over-sensitive was in thinking the water in the wine at the Eucharist has anything to do with 'our'

---

1 Irenaeus, *Against Heresies* V.1.3. Irenaeus was born in Asia Minor, studied in Rome, bishop in France.
2 Mentioned in the Council of Trent, Session XXII, Chapter vii. The chapter is insisting on the mixing of water with wine, but only suggesting two reasons why. In my next chapter I will vote in favour of the other suggested reason.

human nature. It has only to do with the human nature of Christ, since as the gifts are prepared we are presenting the symbols of Christ's body, Christ's human nature, and Christ's divinity. By leaving off the water, we would be presenting Jesus with only one nature – which would be another and different heresy! It is not right to think of Jesus as simply a divine spirit in a human body, without a proper human life, as if he was not properly human but only making a show. Therefore the water is not an accident, it has a true meaning.

So then, we present bread, water and wine, and in mixing the water and wine we pray that as divine Christ took on our human nature, so in the Providence of God the divinity of Jesus may come to reach into our human lives. That we in turn may call God 'Abba' as he does. This is why Christ came into the world, this is the purpose of the Incarnation.

Next comes the consecration of the bread and the wine, and it flows sweetly out of the images already presented. I leave the explanation to the next chapter.

Prayer of thanks to Jesus: Jesus, friend and brother, how can we thank you enough for coming to our rescue. You, like the Good Samaritan in your story, had no obligation to come and save us, yet you entered the restrictions of our lives, so foreign to your own, and took on our human body and the limitations of our life. But you brought with you the ever-wonderful Spirit, your Spirit, by which even you call God 'Abba' as you have done in your own realm from all eternity. And you brought that Spirit not simply to enjoy for your own comfort and consolation, but to share that Spirit with us, with the likes of me. For me this is not just a word, but a whole new relationship with God as your Father and my Father, with the one to whom I owe everything but who gives everything now to me freely. I can serve and show gratitude knowing that if my efforts are feeble or at times quite unworthy, forgiveness is there and I can start each day anew. In fact this is the only thing I can do, Lord Jesus, that is greater than you could do: you by all accounts never had to get up and start again after falling into sin; but with your holy Spirit I can do that. Give me please the Spirit you came to give me and to all of us. Amen.

13

... and Jesus Saves

In this chapter we may take the bread, the water and the wine selected by Jesus, and see how he develops their story to match his own death and Resurrection, his Paschal Mystery. The Spirit has a definite role in the mystery, one move on from the Incarnation and the first procession of love coming down to a fallen world. In this second procession Love is returned for love regardless of the cost.

Jesus at the Last Supper takes the bread, blesses it, breaks it and says, 'Take this, all of you, and eat of it. For this is my body.' Nothing about blood at this stage: the body in question is spoken of as whole, entire and living, which means it includes the blood. Whatever the disciples thought of his statement at that time, they did not understand reference to a dead body, but a living one.

For the final cup of wine, Jesus has mixed in some water, as was customary at the time. The fact that the early church gatherings clung to that custom would indicate that Jesus himself did this. As I said already in the previous chapter, the presence of water makes perfect sense when given the contemporary understanding of water as a symbol.

Then Jesus takes the final cup of wine mixed with water and says, 'Take this, all of you, and drink from it. For this is the chalice of my blood, the blood of the new and eternal covenant.' Blood here, body somewhere else. Blood and water here, body somewhere else. Twenty-four hours later, Jesus' body was on the cross or on its way to the tomb, but his blood was on the ground under the tree of crucifixion, or on the lance of the soldier who had pierced his side so that blood and water poured out. Bread was here; now wine and water. The body was alive, then the blood was forced out of the body along with the water, and we have a visual aid recalling the death of Jesus.

What happened to the equation 'wine = divinity' as we had it in the last chapter? Also, what about 'water = the human life of Jesus'? Jesus did not cease to exist when he died, according to the Christian way of thinking. His human life died as we all die, but his divine life, his relationship of sonship with God, carried on unaltered. His very death praying for forgiveness for his murderers is a divine action. As I wrote somewhere else, his enemies might kill his human life, but they could not even dint his divinity: the more they tortured him, the greater his divine forgiveness shone through. So the blood of Jesus, which began in symbol in the bread and the body, has been rescued and claimed by the divinity, on the side of the wine. The blood of Jesus from then on is seen as *precious*, to use the adjective in the First Letter of Peter. Precious, immortal, not made by human hands.

Then too there is the connection with the Holy Spirit. It was the Spirit of Jesus who was able to answer up to his tormentors with words they could not defeat. It was the Spirit, according to John, that Jesus breathed out or cried out as he died. It was his Spirit that he handed back to his Father in his death. His blood came originally from his mother Mary, but it was blood in a long-promised line, and Jesus was not only the Messiah but was the first to call God 'Abba' since the Holy Spirit overshadowed Mary at the conception of Jesus, and gave him that way of knowing God in his human life.

These realities and truths are what we remember in the Eucharist of today. The truth of God's love and unflagging forgiveness is as true now as it was on the day Jesus celebrated his last supper, as true as it was when he died. On that day, however, the sky looked black, and the disciples feared that Jesus might have overestimated God's forgiveness and mercy. It took the Resurrection three days later to restore their belief in Jesus and in all he had taught, and the restoration of faith was so dramatic that they could never forget it and were quite happy to die for it.

How then is the Resurrection of Jesus replayed in the model he told us to remember him by? The Eucharist is not simply a recalling of the death of Jesus but is also a memory of his rising from death, a rising from death to a life he still enjoys two thousand years later. Again, we are back with the bread, the water and the wine.

When the faithful come forward and receive the bread of the Eucharist (as Jesus told us to), we are receiving his own self but under the image of a body without blood. Here is Jesus who died for us, indeed here is Jesus who died for me. Just before Communion in the Catholic Mass, the presiding priest holds up the consecrated bread over the plate and announces, 'Behold the Lamb of God, behold him who takes away the sins of the world. Blessed are those called to the supper of the Lamb.' The Passover lamb gave its blood, in the story of the Hebrew Exodus from Egypt, to free the people from their slavery. The lamb was kosher, without blood. As I suggested above in Chapter Eleven, this is a form of communion, if it goes no further, that stresses what Jesus does for us, rather than what we and Jesus together might do for God.

Next in Catholic celebrations of the Eucharist comes a tiny gesture which is the first form of the signs of Resurrection. The priest breaks a fragment off the bread and drops it into the chalice or cup. A tiny gesture, but at least as far back as the fifth century this gesture was seen as a sign of the Resurrection. There in the chalice we have, united again, the body of Christ, the human life of Christ, and the blood of Christ now seen to be divine. In a strangely apt way, the divinity is now most obvious, the human nature is there but taken up in the divine, and the body is a 'spiritual body' but there nonetheless. This gesture of the fragment is not to be found in the Eucharist of any of the Reformers, but again, as with the use of water itself, it was the Reformers who gave up doing it, not the Catholics who invented it.

Next comes the Communion of the priest, who receives first the body of Christ who died for us but who then goes on to reunite body and blood, and the human life of Christ, by drinking from the chalice. Christ died for us, Christ is risen for us, and the presiding minister is strengthened to be a good servant to his people. That to me is a consolation for the several centuries when only the presiding priest drank from the chalice: at least the sign of Resurrection was there, even though it did not spread as far as it should have.

Nowadays the faithful may be included in Communion under both kinds, and that is better. All may receive Jesus not only under the image of 'him who died for us' but also under the image of Jesus risen, body, soul and divine blood. The chalice of the divine life of Jesus has drawn into itself the human body and human life of Jesus who died. The net result is that the faithful who come to Communion know Christ died for them, but are also receiving the divine power to love God back with the same love with which God loved them. And as that divine power took Jesus beyond death to rising again, so also the faithful need not fear that death is the end.

Jesus died for us whether we asked for it or not. To love God back in heroic ways we need the second gift of the Spirit, and even Jesus had to pray for it. He prayed for hours on end in the Garden of Gethsemane, and was given the strength. Having won through, he has the gift of giving his Spirit of love-in-return-for-love to each of us who try to follow him. We in our turn have to pray for it.

Prayer: ... one Body, one Spirit in Christ. St Paul writes, 'The cup of blessing which we bless, is it not a sharing in the blood of Christ? The bread which we break, is it not a sharing in the body of Christ?' (1 Corinthians 10:16,17) And again, 'For by one Spirit we were all baptized into one body ... and all were given to drink of one Spirit.' (1 Corinthians 12:13) Lord Jesus, it is your Spirit that makes us one body in you. Because you have shared with us your mind and your heart, and shared with us your baptism, we too may call God 'Abba' and know that we are not overstepping the mark. You are our Brother and our Friend, not our taskmaster or our tyrant. It is only Satan who puts people on a precipice and tells them they will fall and destroy themselves: with you we walk, with 'only Jesus' who will pick us up every time we stumble. (Mark 8:8)

Although we are many, as many as the cells in a body, yet in the one Spirit we now have a common purpose. With you and in you, we are called to tell the world about your Father's love which has no conditions, and his forgiveness which has no limits. Help us to cope with those in our midst who do not want forgiveness, who do not think they need forgiveness, who refuse to forgive their enemies. They, the unforgiving, are the real foes, and the ones you yourself found hardest to deal with. They thought they had effectively stamped out both you and your message, but you still came through, stronger than ever. Help us to keep on praying even when the foes seem to be winning. We know that this kind of deafness and dumbness is only cast out by prayer, so here we are, praying, dear Lord. Teach us to pray, please, and share with us your one Spirit in the cup that we drink. Amen.

14

One Body, One Spirit in Christ

The third Eucharistic prayer asks that we may become one body, one spirit in Christ. This also puts a slightly different emphasis on the work of the Holy Spirit from what we have already thought about and prayed about. It brings together the words of Jesus, the vision of St Paul about the disciples as being the body of Christ, the vision of Ezekiel about the valley of dry bones, and the role of the twelve Apostles.

Jesus was speaking about his body when, as John's Gospel tells us, he said, 'Destroy this temple, and in three days I will build it up again.' His body was the new temple; like the old one, it would be destroyed and the worshippers scattered far and wide, but like the old temple it would be rebuilt. Within three days of Jesus' death, his body would be rebuilt. The rebuilt temple after the Exile was disappointingly plain, and some of those who remembered Solomon's temple shed tears to see the difference. But the rebuilding of the body of Jesus would be 'out of this world', something never before seen, making even Herod's temple nothing but a pile of stones by comparison.

The story of St Paul gives us a clue to the 'out of this world' nature of the body of the risen Christ. Paul or, as he was originally called, Saul detested Jesus and all Jesus stood for, from the first moment he heard about him. Coming from Jerusalem to Damascus with authority to arrest and imprison Christians, he then, out of the blue, has a vision of Jesus which he knows is a vision from God. Jesus is very much alive and asking Saul, 'Why are you persecuting me?' As I mentioned above in Chapter Eight, Saul's first reaction was to start preaching how

God turns out to be on the side of Jesus, but the citizens of Damascus found this change of heart in Saul hard to fathom: he had to be bundled out of the city by the disciples of Jesus. Then when he took many months reflecting in the desert and rearranging his previous doctrines around the fact of the risen Jesus, he formed a whole theology around what Jesus had said to him. Persecuting Christians equals persecuting Christ. Christians are one body in Christ. When Paul in his letters uses the image of a body, he is harking back to the vision he was given on the way to Damascus.

I used to think how far-seeing was this image of Paul's. Science nearer our own times has discovered the way every cell in our body knows what is going on, or supposed to be going on, in the whole of the rest of our body. Every cell is a microcosm of the whole, every cell knows the DNA of the person. When I cut my finger, the neighbouring cells rally round and recreate the bit that got cut away, because they know what is missing. This makes a wonderful image for the Church, or indeed for the whole human race, if every hurt is known and healed by the neighbours. Where the cell image falls down is in the other fact, that cells in our bodies are dropping off and being replaced all the time. If I identify myself as a sort of cell in Christ's body, I could find myself being dropped off, which would not do at all. To that extent the image of family, of God's children round the family table, is a safer one since the least of the little ones is not about to be dropped off from the family. However, Paul's imagery was given to him by God, so perhaps we should simply not push it too far. Undoubtedly it is true that we cannot all be the hand, we cannot all be the foot; each member of the body of Christ has its own task, its own talent, its own place in the living scheme.

And what unites the many parts of the body as one whole is the spirit or life of the body. We could recall the vision of Ezekiel, seeing the dry bones all rattling together, then the sinews and the flesh, but the creatures were lifeless and still until the spirit was breathed into them. Similarly the body of Christ which is made up from the members of his Church receives its life from the Holy Spirit. Knowing one another to be equally sons and daughters of God, invited to call God

'Abba' with all the resulting forgiveness coming from that invitation, we learn to love one another with no questions asked. We are all equally gifted and all equally in need of being included. The whole human race stands in need of knowing the love and forgiveness of God, and Christ's body can show how it may be brought about.

Above I mentioned the twelve Apostles as having a part in the 'one body, one spirit'. Jesus, in choosing the Twelve, his special Apostles, was preparing the way for the coming of his new kingdom. The new would grow out of the old, the promises of God would be fulfilled in a new and surprising way. The importance of the number twelve in the story of Israel comes from the fact that Israel, the other name of the patriarch Jacob, had twelve sons, from whom the twelve tribes of Israel were named. And the twelve stick together, come what may: they are twelve, but they are one. Quite early on, there was a tragic story to illustrate the closeness of the ties. When a woman from Bethlehem was raped continually and left for dead by the foreign enemies of one tribe, her dead body was divided up and a part sent to all the twelve tribes: 'Make one of her body again by coming together in vengeance on our enemy. What they do to one they do to all of us.'

There is a similar and less painful image in the same vein, when Ahijah from Shiloh tears his garment into twelve pieces, then symbolizes the dividing of two tribes from the other ten. The Gospel of John even sees it to be significant that the garment of Jesus was not torn by the soldiers throwing dice for it. His garment, his kingdom, his body, was not to be divided. No bone was to be broken. For Jesus, his kingdom is not of this world, his realm is not to do with hectares and square miles. Every least person is as valuable as the whole kingdom, because if we neglect the least of his little ones who believe in him, we neglect him. If we cut off the least one, we cut off Jesus. If I can only be humble enough to see myself as the least of his disciples, then Jesus will never be separated from me, because if the others leave me behind, they leave Jesus behind, and then the body must be made whole again, the kingdom must be made good.

The accounts of the feeding of the five thousand and of the four thousand have this in common, that basketsful of scraps of bread are left over. There was no shortage, every single soul got fed. This was the bread of the children, each and every one of them able to call God 'Abba' by the power of the Holy Spirit. So then later when Jesus was in the boat with the twelve chosen ones, and they discovered there was only one loaf of bread to share among them, Jesus was astonished at their lack of understanding. One loaf was the ideal, one loaf shared among the twelve of them. This situation was providential, not something to worry about. The city of the New Jerusalem would have twelve gates; twelve leaders who would wend their way through the crowds, making sure all the children were fed. In St John's account of the discourse at the Last Supper, Jesus prays for the gathered Apostles, and then prays for all those who through their preaching will come to believe in him.

Jesus our Messiah, our anointed one, is the one first and foremost able to call God 'Abba', being as he was the Son of God from before all time. Now we are like members of his body, all with one purpose, all with one voice, all with one perfect relationship with God as our Father. The love the Father has for him, the Father has also for us. The gift is so utterly beyond our powers that we can only rely on our Advocate the Holy Spirit when we find time and time again that we have failed to behave like true children of God. When Jesus takes a loaf and divides it into twelve, saying 'This is my body', he gives it to be divided further, as far as the least of the little ones, through the ministry of the Twelve. But always since his Resurrection that body is alive, and the spirit of the body is not just human life, but the life of children of God.

Prayer for unity: *Along with Jesus, we pray for unity among all those who call on his name. You know, dear God, that I have worked for many years in a retreat house, where people come to pray about their lives and about their future plans. When it comes to praying, there is so little difference between a Roman Catholic, an Anglican, a Methodist, a Baptist, a member of the United Reformed Church, an Episcopalian, or, come to that, the occasional Buddhist or not so occasional agnostic. There are many* *things that divide us, but what unites us is so fundamental: we need the adoption that only you can give us, dear God, adoption into the one Spirit through Christ your Son. We all need to rest in that balance between you and your Son Jesus, in the love of the Spirit. Hear our prayer, so that the one body and one spirit may attract to itself more and more of this troubled world. Amen.*

15

Gifts and Two Famous Hymns

In this chapter I want to go through two famous hymns sung or spoken to the Holy Spirit directly, the *Veni Creator Spiritus* (Come, Creator Spirit) and the *Veni, Sancte Spiritus* (Come, Holy Spirit). Since both of these mention the 'sevenfold gift' of the Spirit, it will be well to have a look at the place in Scripture that lists the seven gifts, and to ponder them by way of introduction to the hymns.

Chapter Eleven of Isaiah starts with a prophecy about the family tree of Jesse, father of King David. The Messiah will one day come from that line, and the Spirit of the Lord will rest upon him, the spirit of wisdom and understanding, the spirit of counsel and strength, of knowledge, piety and the fear of the Lord. In most modern Bibles there are only six gifts in three pairs, omitting piety but with 'the fear of the Lord' being mentioned a second time, as something the Messiah will delight in. The additional gift, of piety, comes from the list given in the Septuagint, the Greek version of the Old Testament, which was familiar to the Apostles: there one of the 'fears' is replaced by the gift of 'piety', thus making up the number of seven gifts.

Strictly speaking, the prophet Isaiah is not referring to the sevenfold gifts as being gifts of the Holy Spirit, Third Person of the Trinity, since before the time of Jesus there was no notion of God as Trinity. The Spirit of God in the Old Testament is referring to God, not to a third Person. However, as Christians believing in God as Trinity, we have become used to taking Old Testament references to the Spirit of God and applying them to the Holy Spirit. A brief look then at the seven gifts, which I am presenting in the form of a prayer.

Wisdom is the first. Holy Spirit, when you come to us from the Father, may we know our life's shortness, and that we depend completely on the Father's will. When you are sent to us from the Son, remind us always that like Jesus himself we are servants, and we will not always know why things happen.

Understanding comes next. Holy Spirit, bless with understanding those who try to fathom who made the stars, and where life comes from. Bless those who try to understand the workings of the human mind and body, so as to make human life more like the way things are in God's kingdom, where God's ways are the rule. Bring understanding also from Jesus our Lord, to know the beauty and lovingness of God his Father. So often we suppose ill-will or indifference, because we do not understand.

Counsel is not always seen as gift of the Spirit. Holy Spirit, when we listen to others telling us their story, may we know them first and foremost as God's sons and daughters, with a life and dignity of their own. When the gift comes from the Son, may we share the skill of Jesus in reaching hearts. May we spot good will wherever it exists.

Strength, or **Fortitude**, to use an old-fashioned word. Spirit of God, the strength you bring from God empowers us to call God 'Abba', thus raising us beyond the reach of our own weakness. Coming to us when we pray to Jesus, you give us words that our adversaries cannot better.

Knowledge is the fifth gift. There are ways and ways of knowing. May we know God present in all things rather than know a string of facts without love. May we know God's love behind everything that happens, rather than be always up to date with the news.

Piety is not really to do with eyes modestly cast down and hands folded in prayer. Piety is filial love, the love a loving child has for a parent and for home. Holy Spirit, show us our Father in such a light that we will find him easy to love, impossible not to love. And as you come to us from Jesus help us to love with no conditions, faithfully no matter what happens.

The Fear of the Lord does not mean being scared of God. 'Awe' would be a better English word. Please, Holy Spirit, give us the awe the Apostles and the faithful women had at the Resurrection of Jesus. God is good, God is lovely, God is warm, God cares for me, God will not forget me, God will come back for me. And with Jesus, what I fear is if I should ever lose him. As the old prayer has it, 'Jesus, never permit me to be separated from you'. That I would fear.

The hymn *Veni Creator Spiritus* dates from the early 800s, and appeals to the Holy Spirit directly. Here I give the original Latin and my own rather literal translation.

1. *Veni, creator Spiritus, mentes tuorum visita. Imple superna gratia quae tu creasti pectora.*

1. Come, creator Spirit, visit the minds of your own people. Fill with heavenly grace the hearts you created.

2. *Qui diceris Paraclitus, altissimi donum Dei, fons vivus, ignis, caritas et spiritalis unctio.*

2. You who are called 'The Defence Lawyer', gift of the most high God, living spring, fire, love and anointing for the soul.

3. *Tu septiformis munere, digitus paternae dexterae, tu rite promissum Patris sermone ditans guttura.*

3. You, sevenfold in gift, finger of the Father's right hand; You, duly now become the promise from the Father, enriching our throats with speech and understanding.

4. *Accende lumen sensibus, infunde amorem cordibus; infirma nostri corporis virtute firmans perpeti.*

4. Make our minds sensitive to your light, pour love into our hearts; with your strength causing the weakness of our human nature to stand firm.

5. *Hostem repellas longius, pacemque dones protinus; ductore sic te praevio vitemus omne noxium.*

5. Repel the enemy ever further from us, and give us peace

here and now. With You leading the way may we avoid everything harmful.

6. *Per te sciamus da Patrem, noscamus atque Filium; te utriusque Spiritum credamus omni tempore.*

6. Grant that through You we may know the Father, and through You may we get to know the Son. You yourself may we always and forever believe in, Spirit of them both.

7. *Deo Patri sit gloria, et Filio qui a mortuis surrexit, ac Paraclito, in secularism saecula. Amen.*

7. Glory be to God the Father, and to the Son who rose again from the dead, and to the Defence Lawyer, into ages of ages. Amen.

Notice that the seventh verse is not spoken directly to the Spirit, even in this hymn to the Spirit. Likewise the prayer that winds up the hymn in its liturgical uses also reverts to the usual Trinitarian format: *'God, you taught the hearts of the faithful by the light of the Holy Spirit; grant to us that in the same Spirit we may be truly wise, and ever rejoice in his consolation. This we ask through our Lord Jesus Christ your Son, who lives and reigns with you in the unity of the Holy Spirit, God for ever and ever. Amen.'*

The other famous hymn to the Holy Spirit I wish to feature is about one thousand years old.

1. *Veni, Sancte Spiritus et emitte coelitus lucis tuae radium. Veni, pater pauperum; veni, dator munerum; veni, lumen cordium.*

1. Come, Holy Spirit, and send out from heaven the ray of your light.
   Come, father of the poor; come, giver of gifts; come, light of hearts.

2. *Consolator optime, dulcis hospes animae, dulce refrigerium.*
   In labore requies, in aestu temperies, in fletu solatium.

2. Best of all consolers, sweet guest of the soul, sweet coolness.
Rest in the midst of toil, spring in summer heat, comfort in tears.

3. *O lux beatissima, reple cordis intima tuorum fidelium.*
Sine tuo numine nihil est in homine, nihil est innoxium.

3. Most happy light, fill the deeps of the heart of your faithful.
Without your influence nothing human is worthwhile, nothing safe.

4. *Lava quod est sordidum; riga quod est aridum; sana quod est saucium.*
Flecte quod est rigidum; fove quod est frigidum; rege quod est devium.

4. Clean up whatever is messy in me (in us);
water whatever is dry in me (in us);
heal whatever is wounded in me (in us).
Make flexible what is inflexible in me (in us);
warm up whatever is cold in me (in us);
govern whatever is wayward in me (in us).

5. *Da tuis fidelibus in te confitentibus sacrum septenarium.*
Da virtutis meritum, da salutis exitum, da perenne gaudium. Amen.
Alleluia.

5. Give to your faithful who believe in you your seven-fold sacred gifts.
Give a worthy life, salvation at the end, and then joy for ever. Amen.
Alleluia.

16

The Fruits of the Spirit

The New Testament speaks about the fruits of the Holy Spirit, and these have been traditionally codified into a series of twelve fruits. The sources of the list are in Galatians 5:22,23, in 2 Timothy 1:6,7 and in 2 Peter 1:5,6. With one or two variation depending on how a Greek word is to be translated, here is the list of the twelve fruits.

Love
    Joy
        Peace
            Patience
                Kindness
                    Goodness (or generosity)
Faithfulness (or forbearance)
    Gentleness
        Self-control
            Courtesy
                Temperateness
                Purity

Why 'fruits'? When the Holy Spirit is around and active, it is like being in an orchard at harvest time. Good and beautiful things 'grow on trees'. There is an abundance, and the fruits fall into our lap without our having to do more than gather them.

How I usually turn this list into an exercise for myself or for anyone else is to take it in three stages. First of all, where and when have I experienced each of these fruits in my lifetime, from God directly or from those I have lived with? Secondly, a prayer that these fruits may be around for me and for us to enjoy now and for the rest of our lives. Thirdly comes a prayer that I may become a means of other people enjoying these fruits, now and for the future. Let me illustrate first of all from a few of the countless incidents in my own life where others have given me the fruits of the Holy Spirit.

So, to start with **love.** How could I ever make a list of the people who have loved me? My parents loved me all their lives, my sister too, all her life, and my brother still does. And his wife and all the family, and many cousins and friends and relations. So many have been especially loving, because I as a Catholic priest not having a family of my own, people would take the trouble to include me. And as a Jesuit, a member of the Society of Jesus, I have received unconditional love for nearly sixty years, through thick and thin, from my fellow Jesuits. I can only say Thank You to the Holy Spirit for being around all these years with love.

Joy, now, that comes and goes. I think of little children, and their bounce and merriment. I think of the joy of making music, piano as a youngster, guitar and voice after that, for many years. I think of the joy of firing off a good homily, or the joy of completing a book and seeing it in print. I think of birthday parties, days out with friends, sunshine and Spring mornings. I think of reunions with old friends, letters from loved ones, smiles from someone when I had been feeling glum. Glory be to the Spirit, that joy is an ingredient of heaven.

When **peace** is around, the Holy Spirit is around. Not the peace of nothing going wrong, but the peace of knowing this is where God wants me, and that God loves me in spite of all that may go wrong. Peace drives out jealousy and resentment and all the evils that stop us from forgiving. There is no peace like the peace that comes from having forgiven everyone for everything, and that peace has been given to me.

The clearest example in my life of receiving **patience** is directly from God. For seventy-six years (so far) the Holy Spirit has lived in me and never complained, however slow or stubborn or blind I might have been. God looks out through my eyes now as always over the years, and never once makes any conditions based on my behaviour. Many a human friend has had to be very patient as well – what about my mother, doing everything for me in my early years.

Kindness can be short-term as well as long-term. When it comes to the end of any day, I can look back and see a dozen or dozens of kindnesses done to me or for me. Somebody notices at table that I am short of something, and passes it before I need to ask. Someone gives an early-morning smile instead of an abstracted scowl. Someone remembers my birthday and comes up with a cake. Someone says Thank You for something I did yesterday. Someone feeds me, because I am a hopeless cook.

Goodness, or **generosity.** Goodness seems rather to rest in people, there are people who are just simply good. And they are good to have around. Generosity is more quantifiable, and what a blessing that is: people who are generous with their time, with their skills, with their agenda: willing to upset their own plans to help me out of a fix. A team with generosity is a joy to work with.

Faithfulness, and the great blessing of people who keep their promises. Teachers who have persevered with a slow learner, not gone only for the bright ones of the class. People who have been a support in good times and in bad. Faithfulness comes to light in the bad times. For my own part, I have been blessed by the forbearance of my religious superiors, who have never threatened to cut ties with me in spite of serious illnesses that could have jeopardized my future usefulness. How good to know I would be welcomed back.

Gentleness was a surprise. Whether by instinct or by schooling, I had the impression that a religious life was going to be unfeeling, that I would be a gentle person in a rugged world, but 'thanks be to God' it has not turned out that way. What comes from God is all gentleness, even though following Jesus can take us into very tough situations. As I have been saying in this book, the tough situations are usually Jesus' way of inviting us to say Thank You to God for his gentleness.

Self-control is a fruit of the Spirit. This becomes more obvious when it is someone else's self-control being exercised and I am the one benefiting. For instance, when I am being giddy or silly and the others do not lose their temper, do not write me off as stupid. Or when I am being selfish, and the others put up with me without complaining. In my own heart, self-control is a gift when I manage to do what I set out to do, without being overly upset by other people's reactions.

Courtesy is one of the choicest, sweetest fruits of the Spirit. When people are courteous in shops or stations or airports; when the knights of old are seen as role-models; when a youngster gives up a seat on a bus to an old lady or even an old man; when women with little children are given priority in the departure lounge; when teachers are courteous to all of their pupils; when a six-foot lad helps a little kid out of a tricky situation . . .

Temperateness makes me think of temperate weather, not too hot and not too cold, but just right. Love that was not too hot and not too cold; love that was not all over me one day and chilly the next. I think of friends who have been quietly faithful year after year, not giving or expecting too much, but always warm.

Purity, now, where have I received purity? I would relate this fruit to the previous one. In my life as a Jesuit vowed to chastity, the presence and friendship of someone who is happy to remain warm without getting over-heated about the friendship, that is a great gift and cannot be managed without the Holy Spirit.

That is how the first part of the exercise might go. Anyone who wishes might go through the list and remember many other instances of enjoying the fruits of the Holy Spirit.

Next comes a straight and simple request, a prayer of petition. Jesus says (in Mark 11:24), 'When you ask for something in prayer, believe that you have it already, and it will be yours.' We believe that the fruits of the Spirit will always be available to us but still, like beggars, we pray for what we know God will give us. These fruits are more than we could ever deserve, and they make all the difference between a happy and an unhappy life. We pray for each and every one of the twelve.

———— ⌖ ————

Thirdly we pray to be the means of these fruits reaching someone else or everyone else.

Please,
give me the love to love those who need my love;
give me infectious joy;
give me patience, starting from now;
make me kind, good and generous;
keep me faithful to my promises and forbearing with those who find
*   it hard to keep their promises;*
keep me gentle in all circumstances;
keep your shepherd's crook firmly in charge of me and my temper;
give me the courtesy of a knight in shining armour;
keep my moods level, neither madly hot nor too cold;
give me faithful love in married or single life.
Amen.

17

The Water and the Fire

In my book what is meant by 'The Water and the Fire' is once again the Holy Spirit proceeding first from the Father and then proceeding from the Son. Let me explain.

The initial presence of the Spirit in the lives of Christians is through baptism, which is a sacrament using water as a sign of the coming of the Spirit. The rituals of baptism remind the onlookers and the one being baptized of the symbolism of water, but it is also the gift of the Father adopting the person as son or daughter in the Spirit. After the baptism, the child of God may call God 'Abba' and mean it, because the Father means the relationship to exist.

Water is described in the ceremony as washing clean, as quenching thirst, as clearing away like a flood all the accumulated rubbish of a Godless life; as representing the waters of the Red Sea which opened the way to freedom from slavery for the Hebrew people; as representing the waters of the River Jordan, where the people long ago found a way into the Promised Land and where Jesus was anointed with the Holy Spirit; as representing the water from the side of Jesus when he gave his life to bring us life; as representing the waters over which the Holy Spirit brooded in the creation of the world and of the universe.

All of these water images for the work of the Spirit are gentle and kindly. Washing our soiled selves is a kindness, such as Our Lord himself did for the Twelve at the Last Supper. Quenching of thirst is listed traditionally as one of the corporal works of mercy, it is not a challenge.

The waters of the Flood may make us think of violence, but

according to the story in the Book of Genesis it was in no way directed against Noah and his family; on the contrary they were kept safe, and enabled to start afresh in a world made clean. At the baptism of Jesus in the waters of the Jordan, the appearance of the Holy Spirit as a dove is a sign of reconciliation: the servant is now child-of-the-family, and anger is gone.

The same again with the reminder of the water of the Red Sea, through which the Hebrew people escaped dry-shod, while the direction of the wind changed, clogging the chariot wheels of their pursuers. The people were slaves no longer, but were led through the desert, fed, and led to the Promised Land. The waters of the River Jordan, in an incident that echoed the crossing of the sea, allowed the people on the march to cross through an unexpected blessing. I like the explanation that suggests the river changed course at the crucial moment, suddenly flowing behind the assembled people instead of in front of them. The river does alter course thereabouts from time to time. At all events the incident is seen as providential and kindly. Centuries later when Jesus is baptized in the waters of the Jordan, God is removing barriers for us: the heavens are split open, and there is nothing between us and God.

When water and blood flowed from the side of Christ, that was the very moment when the veil of the Temple was torn from top to bottom, and the Holy of Holies was no longer hidden behind barrier after barrier, but any child of God could call 'Abba' and enter without an appointment, and without first travelling to anywhere special, like a temple or place of pilgrimage.

The waters brooding over the earth at the dawn of creation are kindly. Every morning, to quote the poet G. M. Hopkins, *'the Holy Ghost over the bent earth broods with warm breast and with ah! bright wings'*, and the image becomes that of a parent bird patiently hatching new life all over the earth, in a bright, lightsome and loving manner.

All of these water images from the Bible which are used to symbolize baptism are kindly, and I hold that they illustrate the way the Holy Spirit proceeds from the Father. The love on offer is unconditional, this is what my American friend the singer called God 'coddling' the child. I also hold very strongly, as I have said many times above, that baptism does not call for any response that is not entirely free. All that is happening is God saying 'You are my beloved daughter' or 'You are my beloved son' and asking us to believe it.

What about the negative images of water? What about the violent force of a flood? What about Peter nearly getting drowned in the Sea of Tiberias? What about the two thousand pigs consigned to the waters to drown? What about being cast into the sea with a millstone round the neck? What about the storm that looked like wrecking Jesus and the Twelve before they ever really got started?

Like many of the images used by the New Testament writers, water is pictured as either friendly or hostile depending on whether the person concerned is thinking God's thoughts or thinking human thoughts. Run away from God, and the water will drown you; run towards God, and the water will uphold you, will do for you everything that baptism promises. Open your heart to the Holy Spirit, and you will be God's child. Turn your back, and you will be a slave. (The same goes for the millstone image: Go with the Holy Spirit and the stone will be a support; run away, and the stone will fall on you.)

If water is the image most consistently linked to the Holy Spirit proceeding from the Father, then fire is the image to go with the Holy Spirit proceeding from the Son. The key story is that of the first Pentecost after the Resurrection, when the Holy Spirit, sent by Jesus from the Father as he promised, came down with the rush of a mighty wind on the assembled hundred and twenty disciples, in the form of tongues of fire that parted and rested on each one. We have fire, and we have tongues, and the word 'tongues' is not just a commonplace way of talking about flames: the whole incident is to do with inspired speech, speech from the heart, speech that just has to come out of mouths, fiery speech. As I pointed out above in the chapter about Baptism and Transfiguration, the voice of the Father coming from the cloud was saying that Jesus was to be listened to; then when it comes to our own Confirmation it is the same again: the one being confirmed is to be listened to, witnessing to being God's daughter or God's son in spite of any opposition or disbelief or mockery. This is different from the simple personal belief coming with baptism, faith that I am God's beloved child, faith that no one can take away from me.

According to Luke, the two disciples on the road to Emmaus recognized and remembered that their hearts were burning within them when Jesus, still unrecognized, was opening up the meaning of the scriptures for them. With the Resurrection, there was a simple warmth, not insisting on being shared beyond the present. What we think of as the picnic by the lake, when Jesus cooked the breakfast at the fire and then made very clear to Peter that he was forgiven, was still a very private affair, even though at the end Peter was told to feed Jesus' sheep. The first effect the risen Jesus had on the disciples, men and women, was a rather stunned joy that he was alive and still with them. I would hold that what happened at Pentecost was a sudden real-ization, God given, that since Jesus was alive again by the permission of God, then God was backing everything Jesus ever said or taught. Therefore we are adopted children of God. Therefore all our sins are forgiven. Therefore in the splendid joy these truths bring us, we cannot but go out and share them with the rest of the world.

Just as the water image could take constructive and destruc-tive forms (water to float the boat or water to sink it), so with the image of fire in the New Testament, depending on whether the person in the example is for or against God at the time. Peter was unwise enough to warm himself at the fire in the high priest's courtyard, where he could be recognized, and the fire was his undoing that night. The epileptic boy cured by Jesus when he came down from the mountain of the Transfiguration was always in danger from fire; Jesus said this kind of evil spirit could only be cast out by prayer. Peter had not prayed before coming to warm himself, in spite of being warned to do so by Jesus. I have said before, this second gift, the Holy Spirit as proceeding from the Son, has to be prayed for, because it involves danger and difficulty. To be God's daughter or God's son costs nothing, it is free. But to broadcast it to the whole world that I am God's son or God's daughter, that is not easy, in fact it is an impossible task, which can only happen as a result of being prayed for.

There is a story in the Old Testament that beautifully illustrates the water and the fire, quite unintentionally I am sure but in a way that feels prophetic. In the First Book of Kings it is told how Elijah wanted to settle in the eyes of the people once and for all whose God was real, his God or Baal. He set up a challenge: two sacrifices of a bull on two altars, Elijah at one altar and the four hundred and fifty prophets of Baal at the other. The task: to pray for fire to come from above and consume the sacrifice. The four hundred and fifty set up an altar, danced and prayed to Baal and gashed themselves to no avail, no fire came on their sacrifice. Then Elijah told everyone to attend carefully. He took twelve stones for the twelve tribes of Israel, built an altar, placed the sacrifice, placed logs of wood, dug a trench all round his altar, then poured twelve bucketsful of water over the sacrifice such that the water overran into the trench. Then he called upon God to send fire, and fire came and consumed sacrifice, logs, altar, water, the lot. (1 Kings 18:20-40)

> **Prayer for abundance:** *Holy Spirit of God, pour your waters of love all around us and above us and below us, such that it can all turn into fire, tongues of fire to tell fearlessly of God's goodness. Father, send the coolness of your love, quench our thirst, wash us clean, adopt us as your very own. Jesus, Son of God, send the fire of your Love-in-return-for-love, so that we can turn our gratitude from words to actions as you yourself did. Amen.*

18

A Psalm, and Science

Psalm 104 is a most beautiful hymn to the Lord of creation. It is a hymn to God then known as One alone, who rides on the wings of the wind and who makes the winds his messengers; God who set the earth on its foundations and covered it with the waters; then came the mountains and the valleys, and the seas learnt their limitations. Then the grass and the trees and the birds. God's too was the moon and the night time. Countless creatures owe their lives to God: they look to God for their food, and when it is provided they gather it up. When God hides away they are lost; when God takes away their breath they die and return to dust.

Then comes the verse of the psalm that we attribute to the Holy Spirit, though strictly speaking it does not refer to a third Person of the Trinity. *When you send out your Spirit they are created, and you renew the face of the earth.* (Verse 30) The psalmist understands each and every area of creation as being dependent on the spirit or life that comes from God, and without which they die: grasses, trees, flowers, crops, birds, people, and indeed the mountains, the ground itself, and the waters of the rivers and the seas. This is not about a God who created everything and then left it to get on with things by itself. God's Spirit is involved in the life of every leaf and every insect and in the elements upon which they rest.

This life goes in cycles: things die back, and then they are renewed. The ultimate example of this turns out to be Jesus, whose time in the tomb was a time of waiting, from which he rose in the Spirit at the wish of the Father. In and with the

Christ, we too are promised a new life as this old one fades, a life in the kingdom where love and forgiveness rule without end.

Another reference in the Old Testament to the Spirit of God was appropriated to his own situation by Jesus himself. According to Luke's Gospel when Jesus came back to Galilee 'in the power of the Spirit' after his baptism and temptations, he chose to read in the synagogue a passage from Isaiah. That very day it was being fulfilled: the Spirit of the Lord was upon him, Jesus, having anointed him to preach good news to the poor, to bring release to captives, to give back sight to the blind, to set free all the oppressed, to proclaim the Lord's jubilee year. (See Isaiah 61:1,2 and Luke 4:18) Jesus knowing himself all over again as the beloved Son of God through the coming of the Holy Spirit at his baptism, was full of zeal to share what he knew with the poor and downtrodden, and give them new hope. His healing as we know it today comes from his being Son of God yet willing to share his kingdom with us as his adopted brothers and sisters. We are God's children, not slaves of human expectations.

I put 'Science' as part of the subject of this chapter. Why? It has long been clear to me that scientists, whether or not they believe in God, do believe in a certain logic behind all living things, and indeed behind all inanimate things. They will spend a lifetime looking for a cure for cancer, because they are sure there is bound to be one, somewhere, some day.

An engineer designing and building a bridge has to be pretty sure that the laws that kept such a bridge from collapsing yesterday will also hold good today and tomorrow.

When scientists were coming upon the table of elements, they could be fairly sure the gaps in the scheme would be filled in time; it was like a ladder that would make no sense without a proper sequence.

Once DNA was discovered, the scientists did not need to analyze every single human being to ensure that the same held true throughout the human race. Being human is like so, and we all belong.

If birds could fly, it was only a matter of time till some adventurous scientist or artist would tackle the problem, how we could fly, and come up with a solution.

Humans have been stargazers since the dawn of history, and again it was only a matter of time till adventurers would want to know more and more about them, and finally try to move out from the earth in their direction. The supposition was that there would turn out to be some means of transport.

Again with the stars, stargazers have always marvelled at the regularity of the movements of the stars and the planets. Farmers and seamen alike have relied on the sun and the moon and the stars and the planets to fix the right time for doing things, for planting or for travelling.

Irregularities in the movements of heavenly bodies have given clues to understanding more fully what is going on out there: what circles round what, and why?

So often scientists have been like children jumping off into the arms of a trusted adult: 'I will be held, I won't be dropped.' And I think this has something to do with the Holy Spirit, even if the scientist does not believe in God. Nature makes sense: search long enough and you will find what is going on. I would relate that fact to what was noted back in Chapter Seven concerning the prophet Ezekiel and his vision of the dry bones. To primitive man Nature seemed to be random, just a place full of mysteries that fortunately provided things to eat. Gradually more and more of the mysteries have proved to make sense. And making sense is the work of the Holy Spirit, or at least the Holy Spirit is the one who helps us to see the sense that was already there from the beginning. And the sense that was there from the beginning also has to do with the Spirit, the Lord and life-giver who was and who is intimately involved in the creation of the universe.

Prayer: Heavenly Father, thank you for putting us in a world and in a universe that makes sense. There is nothing worse than the kind of dreams or nightmares that have no exit, no meaning, no affection, where we are just playthings of nobody, with no way out. Always the experience of waking up and coming back from the nightmare world to the real world is such a relief, and 'for this relief, much thanks'. The world is such a beautiful place, but it is not only the artists and poets who find it so. The scientists too know the beauty of what you have made, the wonder of the mechanisms that make things tick, from volcanoes to voles, from insects to clouds, from stars to specks of dust. You have set us a puzzle that becomes more mysterious as each mystery is solved.

I once wrote that 'Reality is friendly', and I am still sure that is true. The reality you have created is not hostile, if we once understand it and use it properly. Reality does not play tricks on us. You do not play tricks on us by way of nature. Always the Holy Spirit you send into our hearts and minds tells us where the dangers lie, and how to avoid them; tells us how things work, and how to get the best out of them; how to keep things going at a pace that nature can sustain, and not to be greedy. Send your Spirit always. Help us to hear the messages you send; open our eyes to the dangers as well as to the possibilities.

Lord Jesus, when after many centuries we were still deaf and blind, you were sent by your Father to re-create us in a different mould. Even though the world and all its people were getting nowhere, you came to offer us a new creation that would lift us out of the cul-de-sac we were in and give us a new Spirit. Still there is a dead weight pulling us down and stalling the world from making complete sense. But the Spirit you send is stronger than death and refuses to be subdued. Please always send us that Spirit, so that we never give up on trying to build here on earth a kingdom of love and forgiveness with no limits. There is so much good will and enthusiasm among the scientists; by the power of the Spirit may the enthusiasm be harnessed to the good of all, especially the weakest members of the human family. Amen.

19

The Spirit and the Seven Sacraments

The Holy Spirit is mentioned in the rituals of all seven sacraments, so it would seem good to have a look at the link in each case between what is being signified and the part the Spirit is playing. Not every Christian denomination counts the number of sacraments as seven, but the processes are there in every denomination in some form or another, and the Holy Spirit always plays a part. The official Roman Catholic list would go like this: Baptism, Confirmation, Eucharist, Penance or Reconciliation, the Sacrament of the Sick, Ordination to the Priesthood, Marriage. I think every denomination celebrates Baptism, Eucharist and Marriage, and there is usually some form of adult taking of responsibility for one's beliefs, of spiritual care for the sick, of offering ways to forgiveness of sins, and prayer for those chosen as ministers responsible for the future growth of the community.

Baptism is the fundamental sacrament, a sign clearly indicated in the New Testament as coming from Jesus himself. According to Matthew, Jesus told his disciples as his last wish that they should go and make disciples of all nations, baptizing them in the name of the Father and of the Son and of the Holy Spirit. Baptism creates and celebrates the new relationship between the one baptized and God. 'You are my beloved daughter' or 'You are my beloved son.' The one baptized receives the Holy Spirit, by which he or she may call God 'Abba! Father!' even in times when an Advocate is needed to help us stand before God in our sinfulness.

The character of the sacrament of Baptism is such that it

cannot be repeated, because the effect is permanent. Baptism gives us a place at God's table, our own place, which no one can take away from us ever. It makes us *this* child of God. In view of everything I have pointed out in preceding chapters of this book, the Holy Spirit in this sacrament is proceeding from the Father, as was the case in the baptism of Jesus. Here there is love with no conditions. God is not saying, 'You may be my child, so long as you guarantee to love me back', but 'You are my child for ever, no matter what! Trust me, and flourish.' Love with conditions would not be God's kind of love; love with conditions is no love at all.

The other symbols used in baptism include water, as we have seen, and light, a lighted candle given to each one baptized. Again, water is the symbol that goes with the Holy Spirit as proceeding from the Father, and the candlelight is given to enlighten and warm and comfort the one baptized, being not yet an invitation to hold it up to enlighten everyone in the house. Long ago, to be baptized was known as to be enlightened, but enlightenment was not yet something that had to be shared with the rest of the world.

Confirmation is the sacrament where sharing starts. Being a child of God is such a wonderful gift, immediately the said child wants to say 'Thank You' to God, and to turn gratitude into action, actions pleasing to God. In the course of these chapters it has become clear that the love proceeding from the Father makes us feel grateful, but that to turn feelings into actions needs a second gift, the gift of the Holy Spirit as coming from Jesus the Son. And the second gift has to be prayed for. A lamb does not automatically become a shepherd. The sacrament of Confirmation acknowledges that God is hoping for a response in love, that I wish to give this loving answer, but that by myself I am incapable of loving God unconditionally in return for God's love already given.

The bishop or other authorized minister of the sacrament makes the sign of the cross with sweet-smelling oil on the forehead of the candidate and says the words, 'Receive the seal of the gift of the Holy Spirit.' It seems fitting that the gift of the Holy Spirit as the Spirit proceeds from the Son should seal or complete the gift already given in baptism. In God, Love begets

Love-in-return-for-love; in sacramental signs, unconditional love from God the Father makes possible unconditional love-in-return from adopted sons and daughters.

Confirmation always comes after baptism, underlining that it is a sacrament to do with response. It asks the grace to love God worthily in return for the incredible love shown to us in baptism. It is not a celebration of commitment: that would be to make a sacrament into a celebration of something human and fragile. Sacraments celebrate what God does, not what we do. What the sacrament does celebrate is the invitation from God to live a life of love, and the invitation holds for a lifetime no matter how poor the human response up to the present.

Confirmation has always been seen as a voluntary sacrament, not something 'necessary for salvation'. As I have already written above, God gives totally freely what is necessary (baptism, adoption), whereas the difficult things are not demanded and we have to ask for them (confirmation). In line with the picture of Baptism giving each of us our own place at the table, the character of Confirmation celebrates the fact we are invited to get up from the table instead of sitting there comfortably, and serve at the table, and indeed show the way to the table to those who are outside and unadopted.

The Eucharist calls upon the Holy Spirit twice, as we have already noted. Once is before the consecration, and once after; once to change the bread and wine into the body and blood of Christ for us, and once to set in motion the changing of our whole human race into the body and blood of Christ in love and unity. The first is pure gift; the second involves us in hard work along with Jesus.

Reconciliation or the Sacrament of Penance features the Holy Spirit in the words of absolution: *God the Father of mercies, through the death and resurrection of his Son has reconciled the world to himself and sent the Holy Spirit among us for the forgiveness of sins ...* The link between the Spirit and the forgiveness of sins lies in the word 'Abba'. The Spirit makes us cry out 'Abba! Father!' as Jesus did in the Garden of Gethsemane. In our case that links us in with our baptism, and the fact that we are now daughters and sons of God, not slaves any longer. A slave may get executed, a servant may get the sack, but a child of the good God will always get another chance.

The Sacrament of the Sick also features the Holy Spirit in the words that go with the anointing. As the priest anoints the sick person on the forehead and on the hands, these words are said: *Through this holy anointing, may the Lord in his love and mercy help you, with the grace of the Holy Spirit (Amen);* and, *May the Lord who frees you from sin, save you and raise you up (Amen).* There has always, since I can remember and a long way before that, been an understanding that the anointing is for the total forgiveness of a lifetime's sins. As Catholics, we link this understanding with the words of the letter of James, 'and if the sick one being anointed is in sin, their sins shall be forgiven.' The letter of James of course was relegated to the apocryphal, non-canonical books of the Bible by the Reformers.

The link between the anointing and the Holy Spirit is once again to do with forgiveness, and being a child of God. In a life-threatening illness it is good to be reminded that we are God's forgiven children. Worries about one's past life can make the thought of death and judgment loom even larger, whereas if the past life is taken care of by the mercy of our Father, then we can concentrate on trying to get better. Here as in every other sacrament the ritual includes the saying of the Our Father.

Ordination to the Priesthood. (I will not go into the differences to do with the ordination of deacons and of bishops.) When a priest is ordained, the key ceremony is twofold. The bishop places his hands on the head of the ordinand in silence for a short time, and then the bishop prays a prayer in the form of a Preface, praying for the gifts of the Holy Spirit to come down on the new priest, to enable him to perform his office well. The laying on of hands is thus seen as part of the prayer for the Holy Spirit.

This sacrament is one of the three sacraments that cannot be repeated, because they are for life. Baptism is one, Confirmation is the second, Priesthood is the third. My own way of understanding the relationship between these three goes like this: the character of Baptism is that it gives a permanent place at the table; the character of Confirmation is that it gives a permanent invitation to get up and serve at the table, and to fill up the empty places; the character of the Priesthood is that it gives the recipient a place at the head of the table, presiding. From the head of the table the tasks are to welcome the baptized, to encourage the confirmed, and to maintain the links across the world and down through time, with other communities.

Marriage. The ceremony of marriage makes surprisingly little mention of the Holy Spirit, except in the way of liturgical prayers in general: Father and Son get mentioned separately, with 'in the unity of the Holy Spirit' added on at the end. This is surprising, since the nature of the vows is very much the work of the Holy Spirit. First Person loves Second Person, and the Holy Spirit makes sure Second Person knows and appreciates the love. Second Person loves in return for love, and the Holy Spirit makes sure the love-in-return reaches its mark. Such is the way of the Holy Spirit in the Trinity, and such is the work that needs doing if a marriage is to succeed and survive.

There is no exclusive 'First Person' in marriage, of course. Both partners take responsibility for giving unconditional love to the other. But unconditional love is what God gives, and what only God can give, so each must pray for it, and pray that it reaches its mark in the heart of the other person through the Holy Spirit. And each must pray to be alert to signs of the love-in-return, which sometimes come in unexpected ways. I do not think the passage about Christ and his Church says anything about the male partner being 'first'. After all, Christ himself is Second Person, Love-in-return-for-love, loving as the Father loved him.

This chapter is long enough. I will not add any final prayer this time.

20

Presence

At the start of this little book I wrote about the Holy Spirit as the eye-opener and the ear-opener. At the heart of things that need an open eye and an open ear comes 'unconditional love and unconditional forgiveness'. Eyes and ears need to be opened to the possibility that the reality underlying absolutely everything is unconditional love and unconditional forgiveness. Love like that and forgiveness like that is on offer from God, and only if we go along with that does everything else make sense. If we can take love as an undeserved gift, then try to pass it on with forgiveness for those who do not deserve our love, then we are in tune with the Trinity, of Love, Love-in-return, and the Voice of Love. 'I believe in the forgiveness of sins'; I do not believe in judging other people.

There have been times recorded in the Old Testament and in the New, when God's presence was felt and described as being like a cloud. At the Transfiguration of Jesus the cloud seems to indicate the presence of the Holy Spirit, and we tend to read that presence of the Spirit back into the Old Testament visions, like the cloud that kept the Egyptians at bay while the people crossed the Sea, the cloud that went with the Ark of the Covenant on the journey through the desert years, or the cloud that settled on the temple Solomon had built, on the day it was dedicated. It is possible to think of the clouds that received Jesus at his ascension in the same way: they were in the minds and hearts of his disciples as they were aware of his divine presence, still lingering after his visible self had gone home.

For ordinary people too, there is a form of presence of God, surely linked with the Spirit, which comes from time to time. We are not likely to be aware of God's presence all the time, our 'head in the clouds' or 'on cloud nine' every day. But for those who are looking for God there are usually moments when God suddenly seems tangible and close, even though the moment does not last. It can be a beautiful sunset or awe-inspiring dawn, a letter from a long-lost friend, a kindness from someone we thought neither knew nor cared for us, or any little coincidence that suddenly gives us the feeling Someone is looking after us. Some seekers after God do a review every evening before bedtime, noting the moments that seemed to show God's presence, and thanking God for them.

Sometimes people tell me how lonely for God they feel, and how seldom God seems real, even though when God does feel real the experience is comforting. But why so seldom? One way I have used, to make the most of the rare experiences, is to think of a particular kind of puzzle found in colouring books designed for little children. I mean the seeming jumble of dots on a page, which if joined up dot to dot by a pencil line make a recognizable picture. For me the rare and separate moments of God's presence may be joined up if we read them aright. God was with me, I knew, at this dot, at this moment. Therefore, I was in the right place at that time. God was with me also at this second dot, this second special moment. Therefore, I was in the right place at that time as well. Therefore, I must have been in the right place all the way between dot one and dot two, or how else could I have arrived safely at the second moment? Therefore my present loneliness is leading me to my next moment.

This is nearly the end of all I have to say about the Holy Spirit, and yet the Spirit is still almost as much of a mystery as when I started. I almost feel like, if it is not too late, asking the Father and the Son to introduce me to the Spirit; but really that is what I have been doing all along. For many years Jesus was the daily companion of my thoughts and prayers and inner conversation; then for many years more the Father, the First Person, the Love that nobody loved first, has been with me every day. This friendship is so precious I do not want to give it up even for a moment. I am going down home with my Father, who ran to meet me when I finally appeared over the horizon.

Of all the images for the Spirit that I have mentioned, the one that appeals most to me is that of Homesickness. I think I can talk to Homesickness, balanced between Jesus here and God at home, calling me home and urging me onward, all at the same time. And not just me. Yes, me, as this son of God, but all the scattered children of God as well, making such a mess because they do not know how to forgive.

Prayer: Holy Spirit of God, balance between home and here, balance between Love and Love-in-return, come and reassure us that you are with us every day of our lives. Give us words, then, to disarm the wise of this world, the atheists, the agnostics and the indifferent. Reveal the beauty of God's kingdom where forgiveness rules, for if we seek you anywhere else we will never find joy.

When Jesus was raised to life by the Father, he brought peace to his disciples. 'Peace be with you.' He breathed on them and gave you, the Holy Spirit, to them for the forgiveness of sins. Peace comes with the forgiveness of our sins, and the peace of Christ will spread as we learn to forgive one another. Amen.

Notes and References

In the text I have kept the references to a minimum, so as not to interrupt the flow. But since there may be some value in providing a fuller scriptural background, here chapter by chapter are most of the references I passed by in the text.

Chapter One: 'When the wind blows ...'

Nicodemus, John 3:8
Innermost depths, John 16:12–15
Last words of Stephen, Acts 7:59
Holy ground, Exodus 3:5
Spirit of truth, John 15:26
Friend, John 15:14,15

Chapter Two: Homesickness

Simon of Cyrene, Mark 15:21
Adam and Eve, Genesis 3:1–6

Chapter Three: The Dove

Jesus baptized, Mark 1:9–11; Luke 3:21,22; Matthew 3:13–17
Paul and 'Abba', Galatians 4:6 and Romans 8:15
Veil of temple torn, e.g. Luke 23:45
Thief to paradise, Luke 23:43
Spirit as Advocate, John 14:26
'Lord, Lord' not enough, Matthew 25:10–12

Chapter Four: True Self

No additional references

Chapter Five: Two Processions
Apostles weak without Spirit, e.g. Mark 13:11;
  14:26–31. 70–72
Apostles sleep, Mark 14:41; Apostles fled, Mark 14:50

Chapter Six: Baptism and Transfiguration

Transfiguration texts, Matthew 17:1–9; Mark 9:2–10;
  Luke 9:28–36

Chapter Seven: 'Them bones ...'

Edict of Cyrus, Ezra 1:1–12
The Spirit brooded over the waters, Genesis 1:2

The theme of this chapter and the next is dealt with more fully
in my book *Finding the Still Point*, published by Eagle
Publishing Limited, Westbury, Wiltshire, BA13 4JE.

Chapter Eight: Plotting a Route

Jesus in agony, e.g. Luke 22:39–46
'Watch', 'Take heed', Mark:13:3.9.23.33.35.37 and
  Mark 14:34.37.38
Testing good-seeming ideas, *The Imitation of Christ*,
  Thomas à Kempis 3.15
Paul jumps too quickly, Acts 9:23–25
'Out of the blue consolations', *Spiritual Exercises*,
  Ignatius Loyola para. 330
Sin against the Holy Spirit, Mark 3:28–30
Archangel Raphael, Tobit 12:15

Chapter Nine: Telling True from False

Ignatius mistaken, *Testament of Ignatius Loyola,* paras 54,82,
  various editions

Chapter Ten: No Exercise for Pentecost?

Contemplation to obtain love, *Spiritual Exercises* 230–237

Chapter Eleven: Bread and Wine

Turning point, Mark's Gospel, Mark 8:30–31
Body, blood and water, John 19:34
'Can you drink the cup that I drink?' Mark 10:38

Chapter Twelve: Jesus comes ...

No additional references

Chapter Thirteen: ... and Jesus saves

Precious blood, 1 Peter 1:19
Holy Spirit to overshadow Mary, Luke 1:35
Lamb no longer has blood, Exodus 12:6

Chapter Fourteen: One Body, One Spirit in Christ

'Destroy this temple ...', John 2:19
Paul's vision, e.g. Acts 9:4,5
One body, one spirit, 1 Corinthians 12:13
12 sons of Israel, Genesis 49:1-27
Tragic story, Judges 19:29
Garment in 12 pieces, 1 Kings 11:30
Throwing dice for the garment, John 19:23–25
The least are not to be neglected, Matthew 25:40
Only one loaf, Mark 8:14
Jesus' prayer for his disciples, John 17:20

Chapter Fifteen: Gifts and Two Famous Hymns

No additional references

Chapter Sixteen: The Fruits of the Spirit

No additional references

Chapter Seventeen: The Water and the Fire

Clogged the wheels, Exodus 14:25
2,000 pigs drowned, Mark 5:13
Peter drowning, Matthew 14:30
Millstone dropped in the sea, Mark 9:42
'ah! bright wings', line from *God's Grandeur* by Gerard Manley
  Hopkins
Tongues of fire, Acts 2:3
'... our hearts burning within us', Luke 24:32
Picnic fire, John 21:9
Peter warming at the fire, Mark 14:17
Epileptic boy and fire danger, Mark 9:22

Chapter Eighteen: A Psalm, and Science

'For this relief much thanks', Shakespeare, *Hamlet* i. i. vi

Chapter Nineteen: The Spirit and the Seven Sacraments

Christ and the Church, Ephesians 5:21-33

Chapter Twenty: Presence

Cloud at Transfiguration, e.g. Matthew 17:5
Cloud in Exodus blocks the enemy, Exodus 14:19,20
Cloud covers the mountain, Exodus 24:18
Tent of meeting, Exodus 33:9
Tabernacle, Exodus 40:34
Cloud took Jesus out of sight, Acts 1:9